Grammar: A Pocket Guide

LEARNING

If you've ever wanted a quick and easy guide to verbs and adverbs, commas and apostrophes, clauses and prepositions, then this is a must-have book for you. Easing readers gently into the study of the structure of English, *Grammar: A Pocket Guide* covers common questions such as:

WITHDRAWN

- Is it "10 items or less" or "10 items or fewer"?
- Should I say "If I were you" or "if I was you"?
- Can you start a sentence with "And" or "Because"?
- When do you use "whom"?
- What is the difference between "lie" and "lay"?
- Is it "I feel bad" or "I feel badly"?

Using examples from everyday speech and writing, this handy book "cracks the code" of off-putting grammatical jargon so that readers can enjoy learning how to think and talk about grammar. With practice exercises, a glossary, and suggestions for further reading, *Grammar: A Pocket Guide* is the perfect foundation for anyone wanting to improve his or her writing and communication.

Susan J. Behrens is Professor of Communication Sciences and Disorders at Marymount Manhattan College, and an associate of the Institute for Writing and Thinking at Bard College. She is co-editor of *Language in the Real World* (with John A. Parker, Routledge, 2010).

SUSAN J. BEHRENS

Grammar:
A Pocket Guide

Routledge
Taylor & Francis Group

LONDON AND NEW YORK

First published 2010
by Routledge
2 Park Square, Milton Park, Abingdon, Oxon, OX14 4RN

Simultaneously published in the USA and Canada
by Routledge
270 Madison Avenue, New York, NY 10016

Routledge is an imprint of the Taylor & Francis Group, an informa business

© 2010 Susan J. Behrens

The right of Susan J. Behrens to be identified as author of this work has been asserted by her in accordance with sections 77 and 78 of the Copyright, Designs and Patents Act 1988.

Typeset in Rotis
by Keystroke, Tettenhall, Wolverhampton
Printed and bound in Great Britain
by TJ International Ltd, Padstow, Cornwall

British Library Cataloguing in Publication Data
A catalogue record for this book is available from the British Library

Library of Congress Cataloging in Publication Data
Behrens, Susan J., 1959–
Grammar : a pocket guide / Susan J. Behrens.
p. cm.
1. English language–Grammar–Problems, exercises, etc. I. Title.
PE1112.B44 2010
428.2–dc22
2010012366

ISBN 10: 0–415–49359–5 (pbk)
ISBN 10: 0–203–84286–3 (ebk)
ISBN 13: 978–0–415–49359–8 (pbk)
ISBN 13: 978–0–203–84286–7 (ebk)

For Frank Behrens, my father

Contents

Contents

A note of thanks

Many people deserve thanks for their valuable assistance. The great team at Routledge helped make this book possible: David Avital and Amanda Lucas in the early days, and Sophie Thomson, Katherine Ong, and the good folks at Keystroke in the crunch year. To the anonymous reviewers: your thoughtful comments and suggestions helped make this book even better with each revision.

Next, thanks to Lewis Frumkes for giving me the idea for this book over one of our lunches. At Marymount Manhattan College, Jerry Williams was a big supporter right from the start. Appreciation to Dean David Podell (with hello to the other Franklin) for looking favorably on my leave in spring 2010. Cindy Mercer kept me laughing and cultured. Big thanks to my friend, chair, and mentor at Marymount, Ann Jablon, for endless support and encouragement. Also thanks to alumni Cameron P. Kelsall and Karina Towers. My colleagues at the Institute for Writing and Thinking have kept me, well, writing and thinking since 1997. New York University's Faculty Resource Network provided the lectures of Richie Kanye. Then there are my loyal friends: Carole Tain Soskin, Nancy Nicolelis, Ann Marie Tevlin Peterson, Michael Kandel, Don Kortlander, and Judith A. Parker (especially for sharing book time).

There is, of course, my husband, who listened to every story nightly over dinner, read every page of this manuscript, and is so wise. My family – Kate, Richard, Shirley, Ed, Jenna, and the Oregon gang: thanks for being there. Finally, there is my father, Frank, my first grammarian and role model for what an excellent teacher is and can continue to be over many years. This book is dedicated to him.

A note of thanks

As for all my students who have helped me grow with their challenging questions, eagerness to learn, and respect, I repay them in a small way by using their first names throughout the book's examples and exercises.

Introduction

Grammar: A Pocket Guide covers the key areas of English grammar. It is intended to ease the adult learner into the study of the structure of English with a comfortable approach that both reassures the reader and insures a successful and rewarding experience. The perspective I take on grammar comes from my discipline, linguistics, which holds that all of us have an internalized grammatical competence: an instinctive feeling about sentence structure and what "sounds right" to us. An implicit knowledge, however, does not necessarily easily translate into explicit understanding; nor does it always give us access to the type of grammar necessary for educational and professional success.

In other words, while you might claim that your "grammar is terrible," such a feeling probably reflects the difference between your own grammatical forms and what is demanded in college and the workplace – in both writing and speaking. In fact, you almost certainly already have a full grammatical system, one that is not that far off from the grammar mastery teachers demand. While the linguistic distance between someone's intuitions about grammar and the standard forms might be small, the educational and social consequences can be great. That is where this book comes in.

Non-standard forms don't arise from our linguistic competence deserting us; we all have grammatical rules we follow. However, when those rules don't produce standard forms, we run the risk of professional and educational disapproval.

This discussion of differences, though, requires an explanation about the labels I use. Most people equate Standard English with "grammatical" and "correct," and forms that deviate from the standard with "errors"; in fact, most teachers will readily mark as a mistake anything (grammar, usage, spelling) that deviates from the standard rules. Linguists explore language varieties – dialects of a language – and try to understand their internal structure. Thus, we rarely label a form "wrong" or "ungrammatical" if it is used by a speaker with full linguistic competence.

The label "ungrammatical," instead, is reserved for structures that speakers of the language would reject as ill-formed, such as *Cat the laptop on the sits*, or less grossly, *The cat finds in the grass*. For constructions like these examples, I place an asterisk before the structure, denoting a non-occurring form: **Cat the laptop on the sits* and **The cat finds in the grass*. For sentences that do not follow Standard English grammar but are considered well formed by the rules of non-standard dialects, e.g. *Here's some books to read*, or *This is mines*, I flag them as examples of non-standard grammar but do not use an asterisk.

Most readers of this book will be looking for guidance about standard grammatical forms. For a fuller understanding of linguistic differences and dialects, I urge readers to explore the linguistics literature. An annotated list of suggested readings can be found at the end of the book. What I will offer you here is a distinction between standard and non-standard grammar, with a few side-trips into why some variant forms exist, i.e. their logic. I'll also comment on how standard grammar rules change over time and discuss the sometimes surprising fact that rules tend to be more social convention than natural; that is, the current state of Standard English represents many centuries of evolution and attempts at setting down (codifying) a system for all users to follow. I promise to fulfill the expectations of most of you, in that I will explain what the preferred standard form is for academic and business English.

I also need to say a word about written versus spoken English. We all know that the stakes are higher in academic writing than in speech, in that a writer of formal academic work is likely to be more rigorously judged than a participant in a conversation or even someone producing informal writing (e-mail, free-writing, etc.). The areas of grammar I cover in this book apply to both writing and speech. While you might be less concerned about the *who/whom* distinction in speaking than in an essay, that distinction is still one you may wonder (and perhaps worry) about. The more formal our communication, the more standard our grammar becomes. You can decide which lessons in this book apply to your writing and which might also pertain to your speaking skills.

In discussing English structure, I hope to deconstruct some of the jargon associated with grammar lessons. *Predicate*? *Participle*? This book "cracks the code" to enable you to see the connection between your own intuitions about grammar and the seemingly foreign terms of most grammar lessons, to enjoy learning how to talk about grammar, and to raise your awareness of grammar so that you can be more mindful and deliberate in your choices.

This book shows why an adult should know this information, that it is indeed learnable, and how it is useful as a foundation for other learning and for better communication.

Intended audience

One important reader I have kept in mind while writing this book is the college student. You probably started college, be it a two-year or four-year program, with little exposure to explicit grammar instruction; in fact, you might well soon be graduating none the wiser about the structure of English. The study of English grammar is relevant to those of you who are English majors (literature and creative writing), journalism majors, or beginning a study of linguistics. Those taking courses in the general education and liberal studies curricula, especially first year composition, will benefit from this review of

English grammar. This book can also work for those of you who are learning English as a second or foreign language.

Another readership for this book is the graduate student, who can also be intimidated by grammar. The graduate school workload, demanding far more writing than undergraduate programs, can magnify that feeling of insecurity. Those of you at the post-bachelor level who are working towards becoming professionals in disciplines that demand academic and publishable writing need to know about grammar. Teachers-in-training will also find this book a valuable resource.

Finally, the self-learner who would like to "brush up" on grammar or fully learn the terms for the first time can work through this book independently. In fact, while I was writing this book, numerous colleagues, friends, and family members said, "I need that book!" Maybe they were just being polite, but I think the book speaks to a need in many educated adults to reconnect with grammar.

Distinguishing features and pedagogical elements

You may have, so far, encountered grammar texts that do not set the appropriate tone for adult learners. The message is that if you have not already mastered the explicit learning of grammar, it is too late, too tedious, too irrelevant, and too embarrassing to learn it now. This Routledge *Pocket Guide* nicely addresses these concerns in both its size and its scope.

This text is organized around the typical questions asked by adults with limited overt knowledge of grammar. Such questions include, "What is the difference between *lie* and *lay*?" and "Is it *I feel bad* or *I feel badly*?" These common questions form the skeleton of the text, introduced in such an order that the chapters systematically work through each part of speech. However, it is not always easy to assign grammatical discussion to fixed categories and chapters. For example, adverbs can be discussed with adjectives under the heading modifiers; they can also be discussed in a chapter about clause types. I thus make use of cross-referencing throughout the book. The book ends with a cumulative final exam, asking you to edit a paragraph by applying what you learned in each chapter about smaller units of grammar to a larger piece of discourse.

Reflective exercises ("Something to think about") begin each chapter, allowing you to tap into your linguistic competence. The exercises reveal different structures in many dialects of English in our world. These exercises also allow you to keep track of your progress as you interact with the material. Indeed, the form we call "standard" changes with time. You will encounter standard forms in flux, such as the waning of the *who–whom* distinction and of the subjunctive.

The organization for each chapter, then, includes a reflective prompt; a commonly asked question about grammar and its answer; discussions on the basics and uses of the grammatical structures being considered; and practice opportunities to test your understanding of the material in the chapter.

The text ends with a list of further resources to explore: books and websites; a "Cheat Sheet" of key concepts for easy reference (labeled Tables A–X); and a glossary of key terms that appear in bold throughout the book.

What is grammar?

I would like to end this introduction, and begin our exploration, with one crucial question: what is grammar? Most grammar handbooks cover what could easily fall into the categories of usage, style, and mechanics (the lines blur). Punctuation, for example, is not part of a language's spoken grammar, but often the first question a student in a grammar class will ask will be about punctuation: e.g. how do I use a semi-colon?

In the pages that follow, I stick closely to the definition of grammar from the field of linguistics: the rules by which the parts of speech combine to form larger units of language such as phrases, clauses, and different types of sentences. (Note: some linguists would actually call what I am covering "syntax" and use "grammar" to identify all combining rules in language, including those that apply to speech sounds.)

I have also chosen to include semi-colons, commas, and apostrophes. These topics are not really in the realm of grammar, but since most readers of this book will be academic writers, some discussion of mechanics is useful, especially as it pertains to how clauses and phrases are combined in sentences. Mainly, I focus on key issues involving the parts of speech and the rules by which they combine.

In several ways, grammar is personal. Each of us has a system that feels and sounds "right" to us. The same is true of grammar books. I have read many over the years, and there are many fine ones on the market differing in what areas they cover and their intended readership. Each, ultimately, is a reflection of its author's perspective, conveying his or her personal take on grammar. This is partly why grammar, style, and usage guides are not carbon copies of one another, and why students sometimes need to look up grammatical rules to suit a particular audience. The current book, then, is a product of my education, training, background, and my own preferences about grammar. By using this book, you too can discover your own connections to grammar.

Grammar questions

I pose 17 (plus a few more) questions, which lead to 17 answers in 17 chapters.

Here are the grammar questions I often hear asked:

- What is a predicate?
- What is the difference between a helping verb and a main verb?
- What is a split infinitive, and why should we avoid it?
- What do helping verbs help with?
- What is perfect about the perfect verb form?
- How do subjects and verbs agree?
- Is it *10 items or less* or *10 items or fewer*?
- What is the difference between a direct object and an indirect object?
- What is the difference between *lie* and *lay*?
- Is it *If I were you* or . . . *was you*?
- Why should passive sentences be avoided?
- Is it *Jasvinda and I* or *Jasvinda and me*?
- When do you use *whom*?
- Is it *I feel bad* or *I feel badly*? *I am good* or *I am well*?
- Can you end a sentence with a preposition?
- Can you start a sentence with *And* or *Because*?
- Is it *I bought a book which won an award* or . . . *that won an award*?
- What is a dangling or misplaced modifier? Why is it to be avoided?
- How long does a sentence need to be to become a run-on?
- Is it *it's* or *its*?

Let's end the introduction with your first reflective exercise.

SOMETHING TO THINK ABOUT

What are the usual questions you ask about English grammar? How many are on the list of questions above? What is your relationship to grammar?

1

The great subject–predicate divide

Take the sentence

Nina, in her favorite flannel pajamas, slept soundly through the night.

If I ask you to divide the sentence into two smaller grammatical parts, what does your intuition tell you about grammatical boundaries (and why they are important)?

Question: What is a **predicate**?
Answer: The predicate is the part of the sentence that contains the verb and everything that goes with the verb.

The basics of the subject–predicate boundary

During grammar lessons in elementary school, hearing the word **predicate** would somehow numb my brain. I learned nothing after I heard that word, and neither teacher nor textbook ever gave a clear definition of the term. If you are like I was way back then, you'll appreciate a basic definition, taken from Chapter 1 of a book called *Grammar*: the predicate is the part of the sentence containing the **verb** (which can be a single word or include helping verbs) and everything that goes with the verb. In writing, the predicate is usually on the right side of the sentence. (The left side usually contains the **subject**.)

While subsequent chapters give a fuller explanation of subjects and verbs, and what "everything that goes with the verb" means, for now we can say that the subject of a sentence is the entity either doing something or standing in the spotlight, i.e. the focus of the sentence. The verb is the word conveying action or some state of being or feeling. The subject–predicate boundary is of major importance in grammar.

Why is it important to be able to identify subjects and predicates? Actually, the subject–predicate divide is something we already know intuitively. Most people, if asked to find a natural breaking point in a sentence, would accurately divide the sentence, demonstrating an internal sense of grammatical boundaries.

Further, the subject and verb in Standard English must match up in a particular way: they must agree. Overtly identifying these major parts of a sentence helps with this subject–verb agreement. In addition, deviation in standard punctuation use, such as run-on sentences and sentence fragments, becomes more apparent when we are able to spot subjects and predicates.

Chapter 4 has more on subject–verb agreement.

Chapter 16 has more on run-on sentences and sentence fragments.

Uses of the subject–predicate boundary

Let's start with the sentence

Nina slept.

If we wanted to divide the sentence into subject and predicate, we'd have no choice:

Nina = subject and *slept* = predicate.

In this case, the predicate is also (and only) the verb. However, we can add to both parts of the sentence:

Nina, in her favorite flannel pajamas, slept soundly through the night.

Now the subject and predicate are more informative. The word *Nina* in the sentence above is the **simple subject,** part of a fuller, complete subject; *slept* is the **main verb** in the predicate. The predicate (remember, the verb and everything that goes with it) is *slept soundly through the night.* Even with this more expanded sentence, we would still accurately divide the sentence after *pajamas*; in other words, between the subject and the predicate, as seen in Figure 1.1.

[[Nina] in her favorite pajamas]	[[slept] soundly through the night]
simple subject	main verb
full subject	predicate

Figure 1.1: Subject–predicate division in a declarative

The great subject–predicate divide

Note that the sentences we have so far been dealing with are **declaratives**, i.e. statements. Now let's look at another sentence and try to divide it into subject and predicate:

Did Nina sleep well?

What does your intuition tell you about the subject–predicate boundary now? The verb has two components, *did* and *sleep*, and they are not contiguous. That is because this sentence is a **yes–no interrogative**, i.e. a question whose answer would be yes or no; it has undergone some moving around of components from its base form, the declarative.

Interrogative: *Did Nina sleep well?*
Declarative counterpart: *Nina slept well.*

An interrogative sentence is formed by reordering the words of its declarative counterpart. Note that the verb *did* was inserted and *slept* became *sleep* in the interrogative. The interrogative, then, has two words that act as verbs. The additional verb, *did*, is a **helping verb** (sometimes called auxiliary); it is paired with *sleep*, our main verb. Together, the helping verb and main verb form a **full verb**.

Your intuition about the subject–predicate boundary is probably clearer with the declarative sentence than with the interrogative: that the subject–predicate boundary occurs between *Nina* and *slept well.*

But what about dividing the interrogative? With the interrogative structure, we have extra parts of the sentence to work with. We would say that the subject is *Nina*, the full verb is *did* + *sleep* (helping + main verb), and the predicate is *did* + *sleep well*. Figure 1.2 maps out all these parts of the sentence.

The great subject–predicate divide

Chapter 2 has more on verbs.

Chapter 3 has more on declarative to interrogative conversion.

[Did]	[Nina]	[<u>sleep</u> well]
helping verb	simple subject	main verb
predicate starts	full subject	predicate ends

[Nina] = simple subject and full subject
[did sleep] = full verb (helping verb + main verb)
[did sleep well] = predicate (full verb + additional modifying information)

Figure 1.2: Subject–predicate division in a yes–no interrogative

Let's look at one more sentence:

Sleep well!

Where is the subject–predicate divide here? Where is the subject? This sentence is an **imperative** (command) and thus has an implicit *you* as the subject. All English sentences must have subjects, but with imperatives, the subject is an implied *you* (it's just not stated); the predicate is *sleep well*, as shown in Figure 1.3.

Figure 1.3: Subject–predicate division in an imperative

Sleep well!	
[(You)]	[[<u>sleep</u>] well]
simple subject	main verb
full subject	predicate

12

PRACTICE OPPORTUNITIES

Divide the following sentences into subject and predicate. (You can check answers at the end of the book.)

- *Have you ever been to Hackensack?*
- *Who's there?*
- *Luz studied law and went to work for the city.*
- *Ashwin, a student at college with a keen interest in linguistics and its applications to real-world issues, arrived.*

2

All types of verbs: beyond "action"

SOMETHING TO THINK ABOUT

Remember your elementary school definition of a verb? It was probably something like "A verb is an action word." In what ways is this definition both accurate and inaccurate?

Question: What's the difference between a **main verb** and a **helping verb**?

Answer: The main verb conveys content (usually an action) while the helping verb "helps" by conveying information about when the action happened and agreeing with the subject in person and number.

Question: What is a **split infinitive**, and why should we avoid it?

Answer: Split infinitives are constructions in which a modifying word comes between the "to" and the main verb, e.g. *to hurriedly race against the clock.* Grammarians have now relaxed their restriction on this usage.

The basics of verbs

In this chapter, we will focus on the various types of verbs we find in English; in Chapter 3, we'll get more into what these verbs do –

what information they convey. But to begin with – and relive our elementary school lesson about the parts of speech – are verbs really action words? Yes and no. There are action verbs, but there are also verbs called **infinitive**, **stative**, **helping** (auxiliary) and **modal**. Further, verbs convey time information, and they do so in ways that require their own chapter, Chapter 3.

Verbs change form depending on what subject they agree with and what time information they convey. This change of form is called **conjugation**. An **infinitive verb**, in contrast, is not con-jugated. *To eat* is an infinitive verb. It is not in any tense, in a way existing in infinity, neither the past, present, nor future. English infinitives are in two parts: the word *to* and the **bare infinitive** part, such as *eat*. (Some grammarians consider the *to* a preposition and the infinitive verb only the part I am calling the bare infinitive.)

Once we conjugate a verb, it takes on various verb tense markers (usually suffixes) conveying information about time and the subject with which it agrees. We have the **simple present tense** form, **simple past tense** form, **present participle** form, and **past participle** form. These forms are shown in Table 2.1 for the verbs *to eat*, *to walk* and *to be*.

Table 2.1: Verb form matrix

Verb	Simple present	Simple past	Present participle	Past participle
To eat	eat/eats	ate	eating	eaten
To walk	walk/walks	walked	walking	walked
To be	am/is/are	was/were	being	been

The term **simple** means that the full verb form is only one word, the main verb. Notice that the simple present tense of *to eat* and *to walk* each has two forms, depending on what the subject is. All possible subjects in English sentences can be reduced to their **pronoun** forms – substitute words for nouns – and contained in a short table (seen in Table B in the Cheat Sheet at the back of the book). Subjects can be categorized by number and person, which is important information for subject–verb agreement.

Singular and plural are the **number** category; **person** has three subtypes: first person refers to the speaker (and in the plural, anyone else the speaker includes); second person refers to the listener; third person refers to someone not directly involved in the communication. In the simple present, if the subject is an equivalent of the third person singular *he/she/it* form, the (regular) verb takes an *–s* ending.

Some dialects of English don't use this suffix, as in non-standard *She eat*. Other dialects have an *–s* suffix in other places, as in non-standard *They eats*.

Notice that Table 2.1 gives us examples of both a **regular** and two **irregular verbs** being conjugated. A regular verb follows the grammatical pattern of taking a suffix to mark tense. An irregular verb does something else, usually an internal change. So *walk* is regular because it takes the *–s* and *–ed* suffixes; *eat* is irregular since it undergoes internal change to *ate* in the simple past.

Chapter 4 has more on subject–verb agreement.

One of the verbs in Table 2.1 was the irregular verb *to be*, which is in fact the most irregular verb in English. (The verb *to be* is often called the **copula verb** in textbooks.)

The last two columns in Table 2.1 list something called the participle. Like the word "predicate," the word "participle" can push readers away. Fear not! The participle is a verb form that comes in two types, present and past, and has particular suffixes and uses.

The **present participle** is formed by taking the bare infinitive and adding the ending *–ing*, as in *eating*, *walking* and *being*. The **past**

participle verb is the form of the verb that can be found when you think of verbs coming in triplets, e.g. *eat/ate/<u>eaten</u>*, *is/being/<u>been</u>*, *do/did/<u>done</u>*, and *see/saw/<u>seen</u>*. The past participle is the third form. Of course some verbs don't seem to have this three-way distinction, as in *walk/walked/walked*, *bring/brought/brought*, and *clean/cleaned/ cleaned*. Here, the second and third forms look the same. The third form is still the past participle. We'll get to the participles' uses in Chapter 3.

Finite and nonfinite verbs

Simple present and simple past verbs are **finite verbs**: their form conveys time, person, and number information. In contrast, the present and past participle forms aren't finite verbs. On their own, they don't convey information about time, person, and number. Further, they aren't "simple" since they need helping verbs to complete them in their standard form and help them become full verbs (more on helping and full verbs later in this chapter). Finally, they are not infinitive, in that the bare infinitive form has been altered. We say that the two participles are **nonfinite verbs**.

Any verb that does not convey time, person, and number information is nonfinite. That label thus includes our two participle forms as well as the infinitive verb form.

After all this, we still haven't spoken about the **future tense**, as in *will walk*. Some linguists claim that the future verb form isn't really a tense since the main verb doesn't convey time, person, and number information. Instead, the separate word *will* is used before the main verb. (Informally, we also have *am going to* as in

Ari is going to walk home

as a future form.) I am going with the analysis that treats future as a tense.

Stative verbs

To eat and *to walk* are two examples of **action verbs**. You can picture eating and walking. What about the sentence *Don is a student.* What is the action here? You can't picture "ising" really. The same problem would arise if we looked for action verbs in these sentences:

Miriam senses a problem.
Winnie seems happy in her new job.

These verbs express a state of being – emotional, mental, or involving the senses; they are called **stative verbs**. They have their own rules of behavior, such as that they can't be put into a passive sentence:

*A problem is sensed by Miriam.

Contrast this with

A walk is taken by Miriam and Winnie.

Here, the passive is allowed since the verb is an action verb.

Chapter 9 has more on passive sentences.

Stative verbs also do not take an *–ing* ending, i.e. don't have a present participle form:

Winnie is seeming happy in her new job.

(Remember that * means non-occurring or not well formed.) Some of you, however, might be fine with

Winnie is seeming happy.

In fact, there is some advertising that plays with stative verbs. The McDonald's slogan *I'm loving it* uses a stative verb in the present progressive form. I recently saw a magazine ad with the tagline, "She's sensing a change in the air." So the advertising world seems to be having some fun with stative verbs.

Sometimes we can have a stative verb in the present participle form when we want to highlight an activity that is happening at the moment: *Don't bother me! I'm thinking* (compare to *I think there is a simple solution*).

Helping verbs

Remember that the simple present and simple past forms are "simple" because there is only one component in the whole verb section, the main verb. That is of course not always the case.

When the verb has help, the main verb and helping verb team up to become a **full verb**. The predicate is the verb (be it a main verb alone or with help) and everything that goes with it. So *can make*, *should join*, *are supporting*, and *did support* are all full verbs in the sentences below:

Molly can make a difference.
Zach should join the team.

Donna and Erika are supporting them.
Derrick and Darryl didn't support them.

The verbs *make*, *join*, and *support* are not alone in the verb. They have help. In fact, these extra verbs are called **helping verbs** (sometimes called auxiliary verbs). More on their function in Chapter 3, but note here that they come before the verbs *make*, *join*, and *supporting*. These full verbs with two parts, then, are composed of a helping verb and a **main verb**. In these examples, the main verbs describe an action, and are thus action verbs.

The sentences above actually have two types of helping verbs: those that are conjugated for time, number, and person (*are*, *did*) and those that are not (*can*, *should*).

Chapters 1 and 3 have more on verbs.

Linking verbs

Take the sentence

Colin is successful with his music.

The main verb here is not an action word. A main verb like *to be* falls into the category called a **linking verb**. These verbs act like an equals sign.

Teresa is a teacher

is equivalent to *Teresa = teacher*.

Colin is busy

could be thought of as *Colin = busy*. Hence, *is* is a linking verb.

Linking verbs can also have help:

Colin has been busy: *has* = helping verb; *been* = main and also linking verb.

Other linking verbs include the words *to seem* and *to feel* (an inner state, not the use of the fingertips):

Andrew seems tired; *Andrea feels sad about the news.*

Note that some verbs, such as *to feel*, are both stative and linking. In English, there is some overlap of these two categories.

In some dialects of English, these linking verbs can be omitted. In African American Vernacular English (AAVE), for example, it's well formed to say

She here.

The *is* from Standard English wouldn't signal much more information. In *She here*, the present tense is implied. This *be* deletion signals that something is true at the moment. Similarly,

We happy

in AAVE conveys the meaning of right now. In contrast,

We be happy

conveys something that is usually true (and the *be* is called the habitual *be*).

Modal verbs

The other type of helping verb shown in the sentences above, *can* and *should*, are called **modal verbs** (some books call them modal auxiliary verbs): they reflect the speaker's state or intention. Think of the phrase *shoulda, woulda, coulda* and you see three modals at work (of course the full pronunciation is *should have, would have,* and *could have*).

Let's go back to our opening question: what is a **split infinitive** and why should we avoid it? Infinitives, remember, are in two parts: *to eat, to walk.* These two parts are "split" when a modifying word is placed between them. So, *to slowly walk* and *to not eat* are split infinitives. But are they wrong? Not really, and recent handbooks now say it is all right to use them. It used to be thought that, as in Latin, the infinitive verb formed an impenetrable unit. We've come to realize that English isn't Latin.

Any Trekkers out there? What about "To boldly go where no one has gone before" as a grammatical structure? Here is a split infinitive, but it has been uttered for 40 years (the original *Star Trek* series actually used the wording "where no man has gone before" and it was made more gender-equal starting with the 1980s series). Now that's a split infinitive with mileage.

PRACTICE OPPORTUNITIES

Identify the helping verbs and main verbs in the following sentences. For main verbs, also decide if they are action or linking verbs.

- *Where has Elana been all day?*
- *Tie your shoes, Morgan!*
- *Maria was absent on Thursday.*
- *Weon Woo is conducting research.*
- *Amanda's been studying Theatre Arts in college.*

3

Verb forms telling time (and more)

SOMETHING TO THINK ABOUT

List all the verb tenses you can think of. What are the forms you are sure of and the ones you can't easily define?

Question: What do helping verbs help do?
Answer: They help convey time, number, and person information.
Question: What is perfect about the perfect verb form?
Answer: It signals that an action is finished, i.e. perfected.

Uses of verbs

In Chapter 2, we discussed several verb forms. Here we encounter a few more and then tackle verb functions. Verbs have the job of conveying time information, called **tense**. While basically we can conjugate our verbs to signal that we are discussing the past, present or future, we can get even more subtle than that. What if two events occurred in the past, but you wanted to convey that one was on-going when the other event interrupted the first event? Or what if two events will happen in the future, but you want to order their occurrence? We can do that with our system of marking verbs.

Let's take a look at two verb forms, the progressive and the perfect, and then talk about function. First a note: some linguists say that English only has two verb tenses, present and past, since those tense markers actually attach to the verb. Many other linguists include future as a tense even though the main verb is not inflected. Further, some linguists do not consider the progressive and perfect markings on verbs to be tenses. These are distinctions about an event's duration and are identified not as tense but as **aspect**. I choose only to mention aspect here in this note and continue with a more encompassing notion of verb forms that gathers tense and aspect together.

Let's conjugate some verbs. Table 3.1 compares the verb *to go* in the simple, progressive, and perfect forms.

Table 3.1: Verbal forms of "to go"

	Simple	Progressive	Perfect
Present	go/goes	am/is/are going	has/have gone
Past	went	was/were going	had gone
Future	will go	will be going	will have gone

The simple present and past tenses, as we saw in Chapter 2, have no helping verbs; simple future has the helping verb *will*.

Identifying the progressive form

The **progressive forms** are made up of a helping verb from the verb *to be* and a main verb in the present participle: the bare infinitive of the verb and an –*ing* suffix. So the sentence

I am going

is in the present progressive because the helping verb is *to be* in the present tense and the main verb is in its present participle form.

A sentence in the past progressive would be composed of *to be* in the past tense and the main verb in its present participle form. Future progressive is a bit more complicated; to signal future, we need the helping verb *will* (since *will* takes the burden of signaling which time period is being talked about), and then the bare infinitive of *to be*, and finally the main verb in the present participle form. It is the helping verb that clues us into whether the progressive signals past, present, or future, as well as person and number information.

Identifying the perfect form

The **perfect forms** employ a different helping verb and main verb compared to the progressive. All three perfect forms use *to have* as the helping verb and the past participle as the main verb. Remember that the past participle is the form of the verb that is the last of the triplet: *sing/sang/sung*. And sometimes the past participle looks no different from the simple past: *talk/talked/talked*.

Again, the helping verb helps set the time frame. So the present perfect form uses the present tense of *to have*; the past perfect uses the past tense of *to have*; and the future perfect uses *will* and the bare infinitive of *to have* before the main verb (all in the past participle).

Functions of the progressive forms

Now we will discuss how and why the progressive and perfect verb forms are used.

The progressive form tells you something is, was, or will be in progress. (Some books call this form the *continuous*.)

Let's look at the present progressive. Notice the distinction between

Nathalia works efficiently

and

Nathalia is working efficiently.

The former, in the simple present, means usually; the latter, in the present progressive, means right now. Similarly, I can say that for a living,

I teach

but

I am teaching at the moment.

To be more exact, *at the moment* doesn't necessarily mean this second, but the usage conveys an idea of some present state.

The past progressive is useful when we want to discuss something that happened for a length of time (progressed) in the past, especially if another past event interrupted the first event. Thus, we can say

Casey was working on her grammar exercises when the doorbell rang.

The *working* was on-going and the rung bell was a shorter event that interrupted.

More examples:

Casey was heading towards the door when the phone rang.

Casey was picking up the phone when the cat jumped onto her shoulders.

In each sentence, one action in progress is interrupted by another (shorter) event. The action in progress is in the progressive form; the event interrupting is in the simple past.

The future progressive conveys the sense of an extended event still to come. So we can say

Dominique will be traveling by train tomorrow.

Using the future perfect allows us to emphasize the progression of the event. Notice how it contrasts with a more static event that will occur during the first event:

Dominique will be traveling by train tomorrow while Lola stays at home.

Even though the more static event also takes place in the future, for this contrast we keep *stays* in the simple present.

Functions of the perfect forms

Let's now go to the perfect forms. What is so perfect about the perfect form? Think of the verb *to perfect* (stress on the second syllable). This verb form conveys the information that something is perfected, i.e. finished. Like the progressive, it is useful for ordering events and being more specific than we could be with the simple tenses.

The present perfect has three functions. One is to express an action that started in the past and is still true. The next is to discuss something that happened in the past but at an unspecified time. Finally, we can use the present perfect when an event occurred several times in the past. So we have:

Present perfect function #1: action started in the past and still true:

> *Shannon has played the piano since she was 10* (and still does).

Present perfect function #2: action completed in the past but at an unspecified time:

> *Devin has eaten sushi only once before* (but the time of that event is unstated).

Present perfect function #3: action occurred several times in the past:

> *Mark has visited the Museum of Natural History in New York many times.*

The past perfect is your go-to verb form if you want to order two events that happened in the past. The earlier action would be conveyed in the past perfect and the action closer to the present in the simple past. For example,

> *Koichi had driven around for 20 minutes before he found a parking spot.*

The action *had driven* happened 20 minutes prior to *found*.

Other examples:

Maran had finished her lunch two hours before she went swimming.

Ray had filed his report five minutes before the office closed.

You might be asking how the sentence above is more standard than

Ray filed his report five minutes before the office closed

where both verbs are simple past. The words *five minutes before* signal which action happened first, so you could get away with not using the past perfect. But in other instances, two simple past tense verbs might not convey the desired order of activities.

Take the sentence

Oliver aced the exam; he had discovered the professor's tricks.

Here, discovering the tricks could have happened during or after the exam. The past perfect tells us that first the tricks were uncovered; then Oliver prepared; then Oliver took the exam and got an A.

When the order of the two actions is pretty obvious, informally you can skip the simple past–past perfect distinction. Even when there is no confusion, however, formal usage would still call for past perfect on the action happening earlier in the past.

If you see the pattern that is forming, you can guess how the future perfect is used: to order two events that will happen in the future. The one that will happen first is in the future perfect and the later one is in the simple present.

Adrian will have finished his book by the time dinner is ready.

Other examples:

> *Adrienne will have given the presentation well before the class ends.*

> *Geoff will have eaten all the cake by the time anyone notices.*

There is also the **perfect progressive**, such as

> *She has been working all day.*

This form is a combo: the two helping verbs *to be* and *to have*, and the present participle form of the main verb. The meaning is a combo too. We use the perfect progressive not only to convey something that started in the past and is still true, but also to emphasize the duration of the event. To me,

> *She has worked all day*

has a similar meaning to

> *She has been working all day*

but the latter makes the work seem longer, and it should make it more obvious that the action is still on-going.

Helping verbs

Besides being in a form that conveys time, verbs must also agree with the subject of the sentence in **number** (singular or plural) and **person** (first, second, or third).

Verb forms telling time (and more)

Chapter 2 has more on number and person.

When we have a full verb made up of a helping verb and a main verb, it's the helping verb that conveys the idea of past, present, or future; singular or plural; and first, second, or third person. Take a look at

I am reading

versus

We are reading.

The helping verb *am* agrees with the subject *I*, which is the first person singular. The helping verb *are* is also in the first person, but in the plural.

This conjugation of helping verbs allows the progressive and perfect verb forms to embody the past, present, or future and agree with the number and person of the subject. Tables D and E, in the Cheat Sheet at the back of the book, show the verb *to walk* in its progressive and perfect forms. Notice that the main verb remains in the present participle and past participle, respectively, while the helping verbs convey the past, present, and future, as well as the singular and plural distinction.

Look at the sentences

I can play the drums

and

Ringo can play the drums even better.

Can is a **modal verb** and modal verbs are let off the hook, in that they don't have to agree with the subject. So we have

Brendan might go to France

and

The MacDonalds might go to France.

The modal *might* doesn't have a singular vs. plural form.

> *Chapter 4 has more on subject–verb agreement.*

Helping verbs also assist in the formation of negative sentences, interrogatives (when the main verb is not *to be*), and passive sentences.
The negation of

Sara is tall

is

Sara is not tall.

No helping verb is necessary. But if the main verb is not a form of *to be*, we have a different situation.
Take

Sara appears tall (in photos or on TV);

the negation is

Sara doesn't appear tall.

Verb forms telling time (and more)

The helping verb *do* is now needed. And it is this verb, not *appear*, that is conjugated in the present tense third person singular.

Similarly, interrogatives of sentences with the main verb *to be* do not need an added helping verb:

Declarative: *Howard is tall.*
Interrogative: *Is Howard tall?*

But if we switch to a different verb, we need that helper, and it must convey the correct time, number, and person information:

Does Howard seem tall?

We will discuss passive sentences in Chapter 9, but let me just mention the construction here because it also uses helping verbs. Here's a passive sentence:

The food was eaten by the cat.

We have seen that *to be* is a helping verb in the progressive construction, but *to be* as a helping verb is also used in the full verb of passive sentences, paired with the main verb's past participle form. (In a way, the passive verb form, then, is a little progressive and a little perfect.)

The active version of

Passive: *The food was eaten by the cat*

is

Active: *The cat ate the food.*

The passive is created by inserting the helping verb *to be* and conjugating it to agree with the tense (here, simple past) of the original main verb. The helping verb will then agree in number and person with the new subject. The main verb is converted to its past participle form.

Another word on modal verbs

There is much variation in the use of modals in different dialects of English. We all have experiences of persnickety teachers answering our "Can I go to the bathroom?" with "Yes, you *can*, but the question is *may* you!" Here is where the textbook use of modals can clash with real-life usage. Below is a list of modal pairs that tend to overlap in usage.

Can/may

That teacher we all seem to have known was distinguishing between *can* as a signal of ability and *may* as a signal of permission. However, such a distinction has become rather stuffy. English speakers often use *can* for permission.

May/might

Another textbook distinction that is not widely followed in practice is the *may/might* distinction. Many textbooks say that *may* = permission compared to *might* = possibility. However, it seems perfectly fine to many of us to say, *I may go to the store later*, with the intent of possibility. And some of us are fine with asking for permission by saying, *Might I borrow that pen?*

Can/could

Both these modals are often used to convey ability. One distinction between these two modals is tense. *Can* = present tense and *could* = past tense. So we have

Rosa can speak Spanish

and

Jamie could speak German when she was younger.

However, both modals can also be used to ask permission in the present:

Can/Could you help me with these packages?

Could is also used in what is called the conditional, as in *I'd help you if I could*. (Some books call this the politeness subjunctive, along with the use of *would* for requests.)

Chapter 8 has more on the conditional and subjunctive.

Should/must

Some of you are probably comfortable using either modal to convey obligation, so that

Sari should finish the assignment

and

Sari must finish the assignment

mean the same thing. You might get a sense of *must* being a stronger obligation than *should*, however. Modal *should* can also be used to signal a warning or piece of advice:

Passengers should buckle their seatbelts.

Finally, *should* can also mean possibility or something expected:

The film should be over by 10 pm.

Would/will

Some of you probably use this pair as a past vs. future tense contrast in the following way:

Donny <u>would</u> swim every Saturday when he was young; he <u>will</u> swim next Saturday.

Would in the sentence above conveys something in the past; *will*, something in the future. These two modals can also be used interchangeably to request something in the present:

Will you turn down the music?
Would you turn down the music?

Some might sense a stronger urgency from the former sentence; for others, the two modals are equal.

Will can also be used to state general facts about the world:

Marigolds will keep deer away.

The negative of *will* (*will* + *not*) is *won't*.

Fences won't keep deer out of the garden.

Would is also used in what is called the hypothetical conditional.

If I won the prize, I would donate it to charity.

Contrast this with a sentence that is less hypothetical, but still conditional:

If I win the prize, I will donate it to charity,

where we now use *will.*

Shall/will

Shall? Is this word used anymore, at least in America? It's going out of usage, but the textbook rule is that it is used in the first person singular or plural to signal future intent:

I (or we) shall be there.

Contrast this with

I will be there,

which signals a promise to do something.

You shall be there,

in the second person, would be a command. Most of us use *will* for either future or intent, for first, second, and third person. So,

I will be there

can mean *I promise to* or be a statement of the simple future.

Since modal usage varies so much, you might want to be mindful about your choices. If your audience is Mrs. Brown from 6th grade, who will resist your use of *can* when asking for permission and instead only choose to hear *may*, then by all means use *may* with her.

Some non-standard uses

There is plenty of variety across English dialects when it comes to verb tenses and other verb forms. For example, which modals would you use to convey the following?

> Possibility (*Peter __ try out for the team.*) *may/might*
> Permission (*__ we go home?*) *Can/Could/Might/May*
> Ability (*Kristynna, ___ you open the door for me?*) *can/could*
> Obligation (*Phillip __ see his advisor soon.*) *must/should*

It is most likely that if you compared answers with someone, you would find a variety of usage preferences.

Some varieties of English spoken in the southern part of the US allow for what are called double modals:

> *We might could help you later.*

Another non-standard form allows the past participle to occur without a helping verb, creating such constructions as

> *I seen the movie already*

and

> *He done it.*

These examples can be found in quite a few English dialects.

Standard American English has the past participle *gotten*, while in British English, the past participle is *got*. When I lived in the UK, I told someone that *I had gotten a haircut over the weekend*. He told me – with a shocked look – that *gotten* was ungrammatical.

Verb forms telling time (and more)

There is variation in other past participle forms as well.

They have already went home

is a non-standard construction – but commonly found – that uses
the simple past (*went*) instead of the standard past participle (*gone*).
In the sentence

Jorge's photograph has proved that the ball was out of bounds,

the past participle being used is *proved*; for me, it's *proven*.

Which past participle form would you use for the verbs *dive* and
sneak?

Greg dived into the pool or . . . *dove into the pool.*
The fan sneaked backstage or . . . *snuck backstage.*

The regular *dived* and *sneaked* are the standard (for now); *dove* and
snuck are on the rise.

Other variations stem from analogy. If we have *sing/sang/sung*
and *ring/rang/rung*, why isn't the triplet *bring/brang/brung*? Well, it
is for some dialects.

Finally, I always remember a German friend of mine whose
English was pretty good but who was insecure about verb conjugation. He finally settled on a strategy that allowed him to skirt
the issue: he would use an emphatic *do* in every sentence. Here, *to
do* is not used as a helping verb but instead for emphasis.

His use of an emphatic *do* made sense when he told me why he
was late for our appointment:

I did set my alarm

and

I did get stuck in traffic.

I finally figured out what was going on, though, when he continued to use emphatic *do* in sentences where there was nothing to get defensive about:

> *I do like David Bowie*

and

> *I did shop for CDs.*

PRACTICE OPPORTUNITIES

Identify the verb forms in the following sentences and explain why those forms are being used.

- *Felix has earned several promotions over the years.*
- *The forensic linguists are working on the case.*
- *Taran was laughing loudly when the children entered the room.*
- *Lin has lived in New York for 10 years.*
- *It will have stopped raining by the time we arrive at the stadium.*
- *Keisha had purchased the computer two days before the prices soared.*

4

Subjects and verbs agreeing

SOMETHING TO THINK ABOUT

How often did one of your high school teachers write, "Check agreement," in the margin of an essay you wrote? What revisions did you make because of that comment? What does the word "agreement" mean to you?

Question: How do subjects and verbs agree?
Answer: In Standard English, they match in number and person.

The basics of subject–verb agreement

Subject–verb agreement is one of the top three bothersome grammatical "errors" cited by college professors in students' writing. While a non-standard match between a subject and verb could indeed be considered an error or a mistake in an academic essay, I will again use the term "non-standard" instead of "error," i.e. not adhering to the structure of Standard English.

What are the rules of agreement, and how and why do users deviate from the norm? Remember from Chapter 1 that the subject and predicate can be reduced to the simple subject and main or full verb. These are the components we look for when checking that we have agreement: it is the grammatical subject that agrees with the verb, conjugated for number and person.

Singular subjects go with singular verbs; plural subjects go with plural verbs. Sounds simple, no? Well, there are lots of situations that result in non-standard subject–verb agreement:

1   when the subject and the verb are separated by other words in the sentence;
2   when the subject contains a conjunction (*and*, *or*);
3   when the subject's number is ambiguous;
4   when the subject doesn't really agree with the verb.

Uses of standard agreement

1 Subject and verb separated

Let's take that first situation where deviations from the standard can arise. What can come between a subject and verb? Parenthetical information, prepositional phrases, and embedded clauses can intervene. For standard agreement, keep your eye on the grammatical subject of the sentence. Here are some examples:

The type of data found in linguistics articles published by professional journals and read by scientists [is/are] fascinating.

What was that subject again? An important point is that subjects are not found in prepositional phrases. Why? The definition of a **phrase** is a unit of a sentence that doesn't contain a subject–verb pair. Subject–verb pairs are found in **clauses**.

Given this distinction, we can cross out the prepositional phrases *of data*, *in linguistics articles*, *by professional journals*, and *by scientists*; thus, the words *data*, *articles*, *journals*, and *scientists* are all disqualified from being the sentence's grammatical subject. The subject is the singular noun *type*, which agrees with the singular verb *is*.

Chapter 12 has more on prepositional phrases.

Agreement: *The type of data found in linguistics articles published by professional journals and read by scientists is fascinating.*

Lack of agreement: *The type of data found in linguistics articles published by professional journals and read by scientists are fascinating.*

Let's look at this next sentence:

The students, along with the principal, [is/are] attending the grammar-bee.

Here, *along with the principal* comes between the subject and verb. Phrases such as *along with*, *in addition to*, and *as well as* may separate the subject from the verb, but the grammatical subject won't be found in these phrases. These phrases are like prepositional phrases, in that the grammatical subject can't be inside them. In the sentence above, *principal* is the closest noun to the verb, but the grammatical subject of the sentence is the plural noun *students*.

Agreement: *The students, along with the principal, are attending the grammar-bee.*

Lack of agreement: *The students, along with the principal, is attending the grammar-bee.*

Having the closest noun, as opposed to the subject, agree with the verb is called "proximity agreement." It is common in both writing and speaking. It violates the rules of Standard English, however.

2 Subject contains a conjunction

Let's now look at subjects that contain conjunctions. In mathematics, X and Y = plural. That seems logical. So

Joy and her brothers <u>are</u> in Oregon

would be the standard form: a plural verb. But what about when you have the structure X or Y?

Joy or her brothers [is/are] in Oregon.

When the subject contains the conjunction *or*, the verb agrees with the closest noun; thus,

Joy or her brothers <u>are</u> in Oregon.

And what about the construction

Her brothers or Joy [is/are] . . .

Joy is now closest to the verb, so the singular *is* would be standard.

Agreement: *Her brothers or <u>Joy is</u> in Oregon.*

Lack of agreement: *Joy or her brothers is in Oregon.*

3 Subject's number is ambiguous

Sometimes we know the subject, but its number value is ambiguous. For example, take these sentences:

> *Either of the books sells well on college campuses.*
> *Neither of the authors travels to book signings.*

If we ignore the prepositional phrases *of the books* and *of the authors*, we see that the subjects of the sentences are the words *either* and *neither*, respectively. But are these words singular or plural? Even though the sentence seems to be discussing at least two objects or people, these words are grammatically singular subjects.

Agreement: *Either of the books sells well on college campuses.*

Lack of agreement: *Either of the books sell well on college campuses.*

Agreement: *Neither of the authors travels to book signings.*

Lack of agreement: *Neither of the authors travel to book signings.*

The non-standard sentences, again, demonstrate proximity agreement, in that the verb is agreeing with the noun closest to it instead of the subject.

There are words in English that refer to groups but are grammatically singular: words like *everyone* and *everybody*. These words are called **indefinite pronouns** because they don't definitely state who is being discussed. Other examples are *anyone* and *anybody*. (Some books distinguish between indefinite and universal pronouns; I don't.)

Chapter 10 has more on pronouns.

A good way to recognize them is that they start with one of these words: *every/some/any/no*; and are attached to one of these words: *one/body/thing*. We thus get 12 indefinite pronouns: *every-one, everybody, everything*, etc.

Another instance where the number of the subject might be ambiguous is with **collective nouns**. Take the sentence

The bowling team is competing in the finals.

Team is the subject noun and takes the singular verb *is*. But isn't *team* also a bunch of people? In fact, in British English, these types of nouns are treated as plural, e.g.

The BBC are laying off workers.

In American English, we go with the singular. This makes for some variation, however.

Look at

The couple is having a party

versus

The couple are having a party.

Which sounds better to you? I'd go with *couple is*. Here's an instance where there is a clash between logic (concept of couple = 2) and grammar (noun *couple* = 1).

Try testing this out on some friends:

The Beatles is/are the most famous rock band in history.

You'll probably get *Beatles are*. For some speakers, and in some sentences, the collective noun takes the more logical plural verb.

Those of you who are older will remember the ad for a Hitchcock film from 1963 with the tagline "The Birds is Coming." The marketing people were having fun with grammar, "The Birds" being a singular noun: the title of the film.

The word *data*, in a way, is becoming a collective noun. It is treated by many as a singular, and the original singular *datum* isn't around much anymore.

4 Subject and verb don't really agree

When does a subject not agree with the verb? There are two instances. One is when the subject is a dummy!

Take the sentence:

There are three tasks Joelle must accomplish today.

The word *there* is sitting in the subject slot of the sentence. But what kind of subject is *there*? We know that we are really talking about *tasks*. If Joelle crosses two tasks off her list, we have

There is one task Joelle must accomplish today.

The word *there* doesn't change, but when we go from three tasks to one task, the verb goes from plural to singular.

There is a **dummy subject**; it occupies the subject slot because all English sentences need a subject. However, it doesn't really mean anything. The verb agrees with the logical subject noun later in the sentence: *task* or *tasks*.

Another dummy subject is *it* as in *It is raining.*

What is *it*? Nothing really, but we don't say *is raining in English. (Remember that * at the start of a sentence indicates a non-occurring structure.) Some books call dummy subjects *expletives*, but not in the obscene sense.

Subjects and verbs agreeing

A variation that exists with the dummy subject *there* involves the contraction of *there* and *is* = *there's*. For some speakers, this structure is invariant, used whether the logical subject is singular or plural. So we find sentences such as

There's two cats in the tree.

In standard grammar, this sentence lacks subject–verb agreement.

Agreement: *There <u>are</u> two <u>cats</u> in the tree.*

Lack of agreement: *There's two cats in the tree.*

Another instance where the subject doesn't really agree with the noun is when the object of the preposition, not the word in the subject slot, matches up with the verb. Remember that prepositional phrases don't contain subjects. The exceptions are when one of the following words is in the subject slot: *all, most, any, none, some* (you can use the mnemonic *A MAN'S* to remember them). These words are a subset of indefinite pronouns. I also call these the "it depends" words.

Take the word *all*. We can say

All of this sandwich <u>is</u> mine (singular)

or

All of these sandwiches <u>are</u> mine (plural)

because *all* defers to the number of the noun (*sandwich* or *sandwiches*) in the prepositional phrase.

Note, however, that the singular status of *none* is in flux. The indefinite pronoun *no one* we discussed earlier is considered singular. The word *none* is basically *no one* (although I've seen its history traced to *not any*), yet it is more and more falling into the category whereby it doesn't have a fixed number of its own, i.e. becoming an "it depends" word. So we find both

None of this film <u>is</u> making any sense

and

None of these films <u>are</u> any good.

Strict grammarians would be happier with

<u>None</u> of these films <u>is</u> any good.

Here is a great example of the standard changing in a very observable way. Notice what choice writers are making as you read academic and non-academic texts. I recently read an article in *The New York Times* that used both *none is* and *none are* in the same paragraph.

In truth, there are more "it depends" words than these five. We say

A couple is here

but

A couple of people are here

where the verb agrees with the noun in the prepositional phrase. Before long, you'll be able to spot other words that are in this "it depends" category.

Three other non-agreement situations

As we discussed in Chapter 3, when there is a helping verb "helping" a main verb in a sentence, it is the helping verb's role to agree with the subject. The exception is with modal verbs. Take these sentences.

Reggie can speak Italian

and

Reggie and Emaline can speak Italian.

Whether the subject is singular or plural, the modal verb *can* doesn't change form.

Next, we have the imperative. Remember that these sentences have an implied *you* as a subject. The verb, however, isn't conjugated into the second person form. Look at

Be on time.

The implied *you* would ordinarily trigger the verb form *are*. Here, we have a bare infinitive instead.

Finally, what about the seeming lack of agreement in "If I were you . . ."? We are getting into subjunctive territory here (more in Chapter 8).

Practice opportunities

The following sentences have non-standard subject–verb pairings. Change to the standard forms.

- *This set of self-reported reactions to potentially dangerous situations have generally been found to be quite accurate.*

Subjects and verbs agreeing

- *There's five letters I have to send before noon.*
- *Jamal or I are going to be called to the board next.*
- *Everyone living with a lot of cats need to stock up on lint rollers.*
- *Neither of the shops hire after the holiday rush.*

5

Nouns and their determiners

SOMETHING TO THINK ABOUT

Does English have different noun types? List ways that nouns differ.

Question: Is it *10 items* or *less* or *10 items or fewer*?
Answer: Either sign will get you out of the store more quickly, but standard grammar calls for *fewer*.

The basics of nouns

Count vs. mass nouns

Some languages have gender markings on their **nouns**. French has feminine and masculine nouns. German has feminine, masculine, and also neuter nouns. These noun categories have their own grammatical behavior, in that other parts of the language often have to agree with them. Some languages, like Swahili, have noun types that are grammatically different depending on whether the noun describes an animate or inanimate object. This might sound rather exotic to English speakers, but English nouns also have categories.

Thinking about different types of nouns, you might have come up with such noun distinctions as common vs. proper nouns, concrete vs. abstract nouns, or even gender differences as in *boy/girl* and *man/woman*. Do you think these distinctions also have their own grammatical behavior? Proper nouns are usually capitalized, and they don't often take the definite article (except for Mr. Trump's The Donald). Other than that, you could put a proper, common, masculine, or feminine noun at the beginning of this sentence:

_____ *returned books to the library.*

(It could be Sammi or Samuel or the student or the girl or the boy.) As for concrete vs. abstract nouns, again, they don't tend to act grammatically differently, so in the sentence frame

Don't you just love _____?!

you can place a concrete word like *peas* or an abstract word like *peace.*

Having said all that, I now tell you that there is indeed a distinction among English nouns that is associated with different grammatical behavior. Think of the word *book.* You can count units of books, so a number can go in front of the word and a plural marker can inflect (change the form of) the word, i.e. *two books.* Now think of the word *furniture.* You can't say *two furnitures.* The difference here is that *book* is a **count noun** and *furniture* is a **mass noun,** sometimes called a non-count noun. English speakers actually do know this distinction, albeit usually intuitively. Standard grammar requires other parts of the language to fall in line with the noun type used in a sentence, something we'll see in detail below.

Uses of count vs. mass nouns

This gets us to our grocery store express line, above which hangs a sign reading *10 items or less. Items* is a count noun. Test it out:

Two items, three items.

Nouns and their determiners

You can put a number before the noun, and the noun can take a plural marker. One grammatical difference between count and mass nouns is in the use of what are called **quantifiers**: *less* vs. *fewer*. The word *less* is used with mass nouns to signal quantity:

I could do with <u>less furniture</u> in this room.

Count nouns, in contrast, take the quantifier *fewer*.

I should buy <u>fewer books</u> in the future.

The word *item* is a count noun, so *10 items or fewer* is the standard grammatical way that the grocery store sign should read. Does the wording *10 items or less* confuse anyone the way it is? Probably not, but grammarians get pretty worked up when the count/mass distinction isn't upheld.

Less/fewer usage calls for awareness of whether the noun is mass or count. The same goes for the quantifiers *much* and *many*. *Much* goes with mass nouns:

<u>Much milk</u> was spilled.

Many goes with count nouns:

<u>Many glasses</u> were broken.

Standard grammar also calls for the words *amount* and *number* to be used differently with the noun classes, so that you can talk about the amount of a mass noun:

The <u>amount of work</u> I have is outrageous

but the number of a count noun:

The <u>number of books</u> I have to read is also outrageous.

Nouns and their determiners

I called the words *less*, *fewer*, *much*, *many*, *amount*, and *number* quantifiers. They denote the quantity of something. Another name for these words is **determiners**. Determiners come before nouns, and they fall into various classes themselves. We'll get to determiners later in this chapter.

Table G, in the Cheat Sheet at the back of the book, reviews count vs. mass nouns and gives some contrasting examples of quantifier/noun pairings.

If you say or write

The amount of books I have to read is criminal

it's not that your intuition about nouns is failing you; the count/mass noun distinction isn't part of your dialect. This chapter started by evoking the grocery store sign (and name of a film from 2006) *10 items or less*. Treating *items* as a mass noun is pretty common. You will often hear constructions like

The amount of people at the concert was surprising

and

Less people showed up than expected.

In fact, count and mass nouns are in flux. Take the word *coffee*. Mass nouns can't be pluralized, but their units of measure can. So we can ask for *two cups of coffee*. Lately, though, English users seem all right with asking for *two coffees*. The word *coffee*, traditionally a mass noun, can now also be treated as a count noun. We have other examples of a noun's status being in two camps. *Fish* in the plural form doesn't get an overt plural marker. But one can talk about *the fishes of the world*. A food store near me in Queens, NY, where I grew up, was called *Cheeses of the World*. Here, *fishes* and *cheeses* relate to categories as opposed to quantities.

Verbs becoming nouns: gerunds and infinitive verbs

Reading is fundamental was a slogan of the Queens Public Library system a few decades back. What is the subject of the sentence? *Reading.* Even though it is in the present participle form (with *–ing* ending), *reading* is functioning as a noun. It is a gerund. A **gerund** is formed from the bare infinitive of a verb with an *–ing* ending (its present participle form) and acts as a noun.

Contrast this use of *reading* with

The librarian was reading to the children.

In this second sentence, *reading* is the main verb of the past progressive, in its present participle form.

Libraries could also advertise their services with the slogan

To read is to learn.

Again, try to identify the subject. It's *to read* – an **infinitive verb**. Thus, infinitive verbs can also act as nouns. Take the sentence

To sing is to live.

There are two infinitive verbs in this sentence, both functioning as nouns: *to sing* is the subject and *to live* is the object.

Chapters 2 and 3 have more on verb forms.

Chapter 6 has more on objects.

So now we have two other types of nouns you might not have thought of: gerunds and infinitive verbs. Both types function as nouns, in that they can be in sentence positions where nouns occur, but they are formed from verbs.

In the interest of full disclosure, there is also a present participle form that acts as an adjective (as opposed to a verb or a noun). Here's a good example of the three uses of *–ing* forms:

Sid is running (*running* = present participle in the present progressive verb tense).

Running is good for Sid (*running* = gerund; subject of the sentence).

Running water calms Sid down (*running* in the present participle, used as an adjective).

Chapter 11 has more on adjectives.

Noun clauses

I want to mention that a full noun clause (a noun, as part of a subject–verb pair, and any associated modifying words) can act as a subject and object in sentences; in other words, as would a noun.

That Monday is a holiday pleases Akiko.

In this sentence, the subject is the full noun clause *That Monday is a holiday.*

Chapter 14 has more on clause types.

The basics of determiners

I mentioned before that quantifiers are words that come before nouns (_fewer_ people, _less_ stress). So are articles (_the_ people) and numbers (_seven_ essays). The name of this category of words is **determiners**: they determine something about the noun. Determiners come in three main types: pre, regular, and post. Table 5.1 lists determiners by their category.

Table 5.1: Determiners

Pre: all (of), both (of), most (of), less (of), much (of), many (of), etc.

Regular: definite articles (the), indefinite articles (a, an), adjectival possessive pronouns (my, your, his, her, etc.), demonstrative pronouns (this, that, these, those), quantifiers (some, many, etc.)

Post: ordinal numbers (first, second, third, etc.), cardinal numbers (one, two, three, etc.), adjectives. If all three are present, they occur in the order ordinal, cardinal, and then adjective.

As these category names imply, we have to maintain a particular order when using determiners, so pre-determiners can't come after regular determiners, etc. Table 5.2 lists various combinations of determiner types, with examples.

Table 5.2: Determiner categories, with examples

- Pre-determiner alone: _all cats, both cats, most cats_
- Pre-determiner and regular determiner: _all of the cats, both of the cats, most of the cats_

(Here, the pre-determiners _all of, both of,_ and _most of_ come before the regular determiner _the._)

- Regular determiner alone: _those cats, my cats_
- Regular and post-determiner: _the five cats, the fifth cat_

- Post-determiner alone: *10 hilarious cats*
- Pre- and post-determiner: *all 10 cats*
- Using all determiner types: *all of the 10 hilarious cats.* (Note the order of determiners here.)

Did you know the phrase *the both of us* is non-standard? Think about the order of determiners in the phrase. Regular determiner *the* technically can't be used before pre-determiner *both of*; order matters with determiners.

One exception to the order of pre–regular–post determiners involves adjectives that convey a degree of some attribute, i.e. when we are talking about how much of an attribute is present. So while we would say

Kenny wears a large coat

and have a regular determiner (indefinite article *a*) followed by a post-determiner (adjective *large*), if we talk about the degree of largeness, we would say

Kenny wears too large a coat

(as opposed to **Kenny wears a too large coat*). Now the post determiner, *large*, comes before the regular determiner *a*.

Even if you have never heard of determiners before, your inner language instinct is probably nodding in agreement to all this.

PRACTICE OPPORTUNITIES

What about the following sentence is not standard grammar?

- *Ryan drinks five sodas a day.*

Nouns and their determiners

Identify any gerunds and infinitives in the following sentences. Not all sentences have gerunds and/or infinitive verbs.

- *Learning to swim is a basic requirement of summer camp.*
- *To find happiness is your main task.*
- *Struggling with a lot of debt, the business finally closed.*
- *The children like to watch TV in the morning.*

6

Objects and complements

Why can we say, "Tony baked Sam a cake" but not *"Tony washed Sam a car"? (Remember that * means not well formed.)

Question: What is the difference between a **direct object** and an **indirect object**?

Answer: The direct object is the entity (animate or inanimate object) directly benefiting from the verb, and the indirect object is the second-hand beneficiary of the verb.

Remember from Chapter 1 that the predicate is the verb and everything that goes with it. Well, what goes with it? Various parts of speech do. In this chapter, we'll discuss some of those possible components, namely direct objects, indirect objects, and complements.

The basics of objects

English is characterized as an S–V–O language; that is, the base word order is subject, then verb, and then object. While subjects and verbs are mandatory, though, a grammatical sentence doesn't need an object (unless the verb requires it). Optional, however, doesn't mean unimportant. Let's look more closely.

Here's a sentence with no object:

Harry cooked.

Here's a sentence with an object:

Harry cooked dinner.

Now take the sentence:

Harry cooked for Fred.

There is also an object here, but *Fred* is a different type of object from *dinner*. In our sentences above, *dinner* is the **direct object** (DO), directly receiving the action; *Fred* is the **indirect object** (IO), benefiting from the action in a more second-hand way. And we can construct a sentence with both types of objects:

Harry cooked dinner for Fred.

Here the order is S–V–DO–IO.

Why should we care about objects? As we see with the sentence pair that started this chapter, English allows us to move objects around, but in a limited way. Those movement possibilities depend on the sentence's main verb and on the objects.

Uses of objects

Let's compare the verbs *to bake* and *to cook*:

Tony baked a cake for Sam

and

Tony baked Sam a cake.

These sentences show that *to bake* lets the DO (*a cake*) and IO (*Sam*) be in either order. (Note that when the IO is first, there is no preposition. Some linguists call this the "double object construction.")

The sentence pair

Harry cooked dinner for Fred

and

Harry cooked Fred dinner

also shows a verb (*to cook*) allowing the DO (*dinner*) and IO (*Fred*) to be in either order.

But the story is different with

Tony washed the car for Sam,

which sounds fine, and

**Tony washed Sam the car*

which does not. The same order of IO (*Sam*) before DO (*the car*) – the double object construction – doesn't work here. Why not? It is all in the verb *to wash*.

Some main verbs allow this switching of object order and some don't. Traditional linguistic theory says that the basic structure of a sentence is DO and then IO. If we can move the IO earlier in the sentence (and delete the preposition), we have done what is called **dative movement**.

Linguists are actually still working on figuring out the commonality of verbs that allow dative movement and those that do not. (In fact, dative movement is a rather traditional analysis; much current literature tries to explain the double object construction – where IO precedes DO – in different ways, without consensus. For our purposes, however, dative movement is a useful explanation.)

Our own intuitions don't need to work out any of this: we automatically reject dative movement with *to wash* (that is to say, we wouldn't judge as well formed the sentences with asterisks in this chapter).

Let's go back to Tony and Sam (I love thinking about men cooking and baking). We accept the sentences

Tony baked a cake for Sam

and

Tony baked Sam a cake.

Suppose *a cake* is changed to its pronoun form:

Tony baked it for Sam.

Still okay, but now try dative movement and we get

*Tony baked Sam it.

The verb *to bake* is now unhappy with the indirect object coming before the direct object. The only difference is that the direct object is a pronoun. This is another restriction on dative movement. Note how much you know about the interaction of verbs and objects already, in that you automatically accept or reject grammatical forms, even though you might not be familiar with the linguistic terminology.

Objects and complements

Let's now take this sentence:

Harry cooked dinner for the weekend.

Does *the weekend* benefit from the cooking? Not really. If *the weekend* isn't the IO, what is it? *For the weekend* is a prepositional phrase, and thus it includes a different type of object. *The weekend* is the object of the preposition (we could also say it is the object *in* the prepositional phrase).

> *Chapter 12 has more on prepositional phrases.*

Here's a summary of the various behaviors of DO and IO:

Base form:

> *Tony baked a cake for Sam*: DO, then IO

Dative movement allowed (double object construction):

> *Tony baked Sam a cake*: IO before DO

Dative movement not allowed:

> *Tony washed the car for Sam*: DO before IO
> **Tony washed Sam the car*: can't have IO before DO
> **Tony baked Sam it*: DO is a pronoun

IO is also object of preposition:

> *Tony washed the car for Sam.*
> *Harry cooked dinner for Fred.*
> *Mathilda danced for the audience.*

No IO; only object of preposition:

> *Harry cooked dinner for the weekend.*
> *Beth read the book on the subway.*

No DO; only IO (with preposition):

> *Harry cooked for Fred.*

No DO; only IO (without preposition):

> *Harry texted Fred.*

Back to gerunds and infinitive verbs

In Chapter 5, we discussed gerunds and infinitive verbs acting as nouns. We return briefly to them here because verbs are sometimes choosy about whether a gerund or infinitive can act as a direct object (DO). (Of course what I mean by verbs being choosy is that standard grammar has evolved so that some verbs take gerunds and some take infinitives as their DO.) We can say

> *I enjoy traveling*

where the direct object is a gerund. It is not Standard English, however, to say

> *I enjoy to travel.*

(Some English dialects do allow it. However, my word-processing grammar checker just flagged the sample sentence above. Not surprising: grammar checkers are programmed with standard rules.)

To enjoy, then, chooses gerund and not infinitive as its direct object preference.

The opposite is true for the verb *to want*:

I want to travel (not **I want traveling*).

To want chooses infinitive and not gerund as its direct object.

Some verbs don't care!

I like traveling

and

I like to travel

are equally standard. Part of our inner competence about English tells us what sounds "right." As I note above, though, there are dialectal differences in gerund and infinitive use.

The basics of complements

Another structure that can be found in the predicate – but is not a DO or IO or prepositional phrase – is called a **complement**, and there are various types. Take the sentence

Ali is fabulous.

The predicate, *is fabulous*, contains no objects or prepositional phrases. And remember that the verb used here is a linking verb, so we can think of this sentence as

Ali = fabulous.

Chapter 11 will cover adjectives, but you probably already know that the word *fabulous* is a description word, hence an adjective. What we have here after the verb is a complement; further, this type of complement is an adjective and it describes the subject. It is a **subject complement of the adjectival type**. Subject complements are found when the sentence contains a linking verb.

Keen readers will anticipate this next part. There is another type of subject complement:

Allen is a mathematician.

Here, the linking verb is followed by a noun, not an adjective, but the predicate still contains a subject complement. Thus, this sentence contains a **subject complement of the noun phrase type**. Another way to say this is that subject complements can be "predicate adjectives" or "predicate nouns," i.e. in the predicate.

Okay so far? (I always find all these complements mind-boggling.) Let's now look at material in the predicate that relates to a direct object, not to a subject.

Shelby considers her friends loyal.

The predicate is *considers her friends loyal*: *considers* = verb; *her friends* = direct object; *loyal* = adjective describing direct object. *Loyal* is a **direct object complement of the adjectival type**. And there can be **direct object complements of the noun phrase type**:

Jerry appointed the shy student attendance monitor.

The complement *attendance monitor* relates to the direct object *the shy student*.

Objects and complements

Note that you can insert *to be* before a direct object complement:

Shelby considers her friends (to be) loyal.
Jerry appointed the shy student (to be) attendance monitor.

Direct object complements, then, just like subject complements, can be predicate adjectives or predicate nouns.

To help you sort all this out, Tables J and K (in the Cheat Sheet at the back of the book) list complements by which part of the sentence is being described (subject or direct object) and by the part of speech in the complement position (noun or adjective), respectively.

Some grammar books broaden the category of complement to include other parts of speech. What we have here gives you a sane overview.

PRACTICE OPPORTUNITIES

Identify any direct and indirect objects in the following sentences.

- *Felicia sent a letter to Janna.*
- *Janna gave Taylor the letter next.*
- *Taylor read the letter on the bus.*

Can dative movement happen in the sentences above to give you the double object construction?

Do the following sentences contain complements? If so, what types?

- *Chris thought the children bright.*
- *Chris taught the children music.*
- *Chris seems to be a patient teacher.*

7

Verb transitivity

SOMETHING TO THINK ABOUT

Consider the grammaticality of the following sentence: "I am going to lay in the sun."

Question: What is the difference between *lie* and *lay*?
Answer: *Lie* does not take a direct object; *lay* requires a direct object.

The basics of transitivity

In Chapter 6, we looked at objects. This chapter explores the way objects interact with verbs. There are certain verbs that are "choosy" about whether or not they allow objects to follow them in the predicate. (Did you know verbs were so picky? As I said earlier, the verbs themselves don't care; Standard English and most dialects agree on verbs and what objects follow, but again there is dialectal variety.)

Take the sentence

Fiona finds.

Now there is a sentence everyone would agree is not well formed, i.e. needs an asterisk in front of it! It's not a matter of standard or non-standard; the sentence would be rejected by our linguistic competence as not complete. You are probably thinking, "Something is missing; she finds what?" It's the direct object that is missing. The verb *to find* requires a direct object in the predicate; without it, the structure is ungrammatical. Going back to Fiona, take instead

Fiona puts.

Again, you know something is missing, and you might even now know to say, "the direct object." But

Fiona puts the crystal ball

still isn't grammatical. The verb *to put* requires more than a direct object in the predicate: she has to put something somewhere. We need a prepositional phrase giving us location information.

Verbs that require direct objects (DO) are called **transitive verbs**. The verb *to find* is transitive. Those that require two objects are called **ditransitive**. The verb *to put* is ditransitive, needing both a DO and an object in a prepositional phrase, in this case signaling the target location. Fiona has to put something somewhere for the sentence to be complete.

Some verbs are not obligatorily ditransitive but can be used that way, as in

Shaun answered the question in the exam

which has both a DO (*the question*) and an object in the prepositional phrase (*the exam*). *To answer*, however, can also appear with only one or even no object:

Shaun answered the question.
Shaun answered correctly.

Verb transitivity

And I am sure you are with me on this: some verbs don't allow direct objects at all. These types of verbs are called **intransitive verbs**.

Nina slept,

for example, would not be well formed with a direct object, such as

*Nina slept the futon.

(There are some idiomatic expressions such as *Nina slept the night,* however.) *To sleep* is an intransitive verb.

Some verbs can be used in either a transitive or an intransitive way. *To eat,* for example, has a transitive use:

Shirley ate the jelly beans

and an intransitive use:

Shirley ate.

Intransitive verbs, while they don't allow direct objects, can be followed by other types of objects. So we can have

Shirley shopped (no object at all),
Shirley shopped for Ed (*Ed* = indirect object), and
Shirley shopped for hours (*hours* = object of preposition).

Some dialects, although not standard, allow

Shirley shopped Macy's (*Macy's* = DO).

This could also be interpreted as reduced from *at Macy's*. When I moved to Brooklyn, the local shopping strip displayed banners that read *Shop the New Smith Street.*

Uses of transitivity

Let's go back to our pair *lie/lay* from the opening question. Some hesitate when choosing between these verbs. Why? Well, their meaning is similar; further, when the two verbs are conjugated, the past tense form of one looks like the present tense form of the other. Finally, there are two meanings of the verb *to lie*. The grammatical key to sorting this out is that *to lie* is intransitive and *to lay* is transitive.

Table 7.1 to the rescue. This table lists the verb-form triplets for these verbs.

Table 7.1: Verb forms of to lie and to lay

Infinitive	Simple present/simple past/past participle
To lie	lie(s)/lay/lain = intransitive (place oneself parallel to a surface)
To lay	lay(s)/laid/laid = transitive (place something down)
To lie	lie(s)/lied/lied = intransitive (not tell the truth)

(To lie) Mei the cat lies in the sun. Yesterday she lay in the sun. She has lain in the sun every day for a week.

(To lay) The owner lays Mei's food on the counter. He laid the food on the counter yesterday. He has laid the food on the counter every day for a week.

(The other to lie) He lies to Mei. I lied once to a cat. I have lied enough to know you can't get away with it.

Go back to our opening sentence

I am going to lay in the sun.

The verb *to lay* is transitive but is not supplied with a direct object. Thus, the standard form would be

I am going to <u>lie</u> in the sun.

For many, though, _lay in the sun_ is a fixed form; it sounds better and means _sun oneself_. It is a non-standard use of the verb, though.

There is variation in transitivity across English users. Here are some other transitivity pairings that can be confusing when trying to master Standard English and that vary across English dialects.

Sit/set

Sit in the chair (to sit is intransitive, so no DO) and
Set the table (to set is transitive, so there needs to be a DO).

Some dialects will ask a guest to _set a while_ (_set_ being used in an intransitive form). We can also find the structure _I will set me down_, where _set_ is indeed followed by a DO (_me_), but one that standard speakers wouldn't use, choosing instead the intransitive _sit_.

Rise/raise

I rise from my seat.
I raise my hand.

Rise is intransitive (no DO) and _raise_ is something you do to something else (the DO), hence transitive.

Here are the verbs in triplets, in their present, past, and past participle forms:

Rise (intransitive): _Today I rise at 6 am. Yesterday I rose at 6 am. I have risen at 6 am every day this week._

Raise (transitive): _Today I raise the issue. Yesterday I raised the issue. I have raised the issue three times now._

These verbs also occur in noun forms: a _raise_ = increase in salary (in American English), and a _rise_ is used in the expression _get a rise_ *out of the crowd*, meaning to anger. Here's a variation: I was watching a British sitcom called *The IT Crowd*, and the tech support characters were all excited about rumors of a "pay rise." So here is a dialect difference across the pond.

Those of us who have to stop and think, *Is it lie or lay? Rise or raise?* are wrestling with verbs that differ in transitivity.

PRACTICE OPPORTUNITIES

The following sentences include non-standard uses of verbs. Discuss what is non-standard about their use.

- *The plan impacts our economy.*
- *Harriet graduated high school last year.*
- *Marsha laid on the couch yesterday, doing nothing.*

8

The subjunctive:
in the right mood

SOMETHING TO THINK ABOUT

What are your associations with the word **subjunctive**, perhaps from high school English or studying a foreign language?

Question: Is it *If I were you* or . . . *was you*?
Answer: *If I were you*, unless in reality you could be someone else!

The basics of the subjunctive mood

Does the word **subjunctive** either terrify you or make you glaze over? Have you read somewhere that "the subjunctive is dead" and either rejoiced or mourned (or glazed over)? Here are some important facts: (1) the subjunctive is a **mood**, not a tense (some books call it a "mode," as in modal verbs; we'll see the connection later); (2) it is indeed disappearing for many English users; and (3) it pops up in seemingly arbitrary places. While the subjunctive is thus hard to pin down, it's worth exploring as part of our increased awareness of grammar.

Mood is the distinction we work with when we differentiate among: stating a fact; issuing a command; exclaiming something;

asking a question; and talking about an impossibility, something in doubt, or something to be wished for.

There are five moods.

- The declarative sentence

  Jill loves the theater

  is in the **indicative mood**. This sentence states a fact.

- The command

  Jill, see the director right away

  uses the **imperative mood**, issuing a directive.

- The exclamation

  She is so talented!

  uses the **exclamatory mood**; the speaker is proclaiming something. Note the exclamation point.

- The question

  Did Jill pass the audition?

  is in the **interrogative mood**.

- The mood used to convey something impossible, hypothetical, or wishful,

  If I were you, I'd tell the truth,

  is the **subjunctive mood**.

This chapter will focus on the last mood: the subjunctive.

The seeming mismatch of *I* and *were* in *if I were you* signals that we are dealing with the subjunctive mood. Other clues to the subjunctive include the use of bare infinitive verbs, certain modal verbs, and the *if/then* construction. Let's now look at how English uses the subjunctive.

Uses of the subjunctive

The subjunctive mood is used to convey the following meanings:

- Contrary to fact or hypothetical –

  If I <u>were</u> you, I would go home. <u>Were</u> it not for his dog, David would never take walks.

- Something in doubt –

  If this treaty <u>were</u> signed, there would be peace.

  Compare to the more likely-to-happen

  If this treaty is signed, there will be peace

  which is not in the subjunctive mood.

- Something for which you are (or were, or will be) wishing –

  I asked that Corinne <u>be</u> here by 9 am.

- In idioms –

  If need <u>be</u>; far <u>be</u> it from me.

The subjunctive mood is frequently signaled by the form of the verb *to be*. We see above that the subjunctive can be formed with either the verb form *were* or the bare infinitive *be* (without the *to*), regardless of the subject of the sentence.

We can also put other verbs besides *to be* in the subjunctive form:

I demand that she <u>see</u> her advisor right away.

Here the verb *see* is unconjugated, i.e. in the bare infinitive. Further, not all sentences with subjunctive verb forms start with *if*.

The subjunctive: in the right mood

Were Jane Austen still writing today, she'd approve of all these zombie books.

(Not all sentences starting with *if* are in the subjunctive mood either; see below.)

The subjunctive mood overlaps with meanings that are "conditional" and "hypothetical." (Some books say the subjunctive is one kind of conditional; I am going with subjunctive being the larger category. Or more specifically, the meaning of a sentence can be conditional or hypothetical, but the verb form is in the subjunctive mood.)

Conditional conveys possibility, but not assurance that something will happen; something depends on something else happening. Conditional can be thought of as an *if/then* scenario. Further, there are two subsets to the conditional: one hypothetical, one not.

- **Hypothetical conditional**: this meaning is conveyed by the formula: *if* + past tense of verb + modal verb *would/could/might* + bare infinitive . . .

  If he went to the party, then he would bring some cake.

In this sentence, the first clause is hypothetical – hasn't happened yet and might not ever happen; the second clause is conditional – he'd only do the second action if he did the first one stated. It is not likely that he is going to go to the party, according to this sentence. In general, if (and only if) Event A is to happen, then Event B would also happen.

- **Conditional**: here the meaning is still conditional (*if/then*) but less hypothetical. We use the formula *if* + present tense of verb + modal verb w*ill* + bare infinitive . . .

  If he goes to the party, then he will bring some cake.

The subjunctive: in the right mood

In this sentence, our man is more likely to attend the party than in the hypothetical conditional sentence.

The conditional sentences here aren't employing a subjunctive verb form, but they are using modal verbs (modal as in mode as in mood).

Chapters 2 and 3 have more on modal verbs.

They could, however, use subjunctive verb forms. Here is a sentence with a hypothetical conditional meaning but no *if* . . .

What would you buy <u>were</u> you to win the lottery?

One more related structure is the **hypothetical future**. This sentence has no *if* clause, but it uses the modals *could* or *would* to convey something possible in the future:

What <u>would</u> you buy with a million dollars?
I wish I <u>could</u> win that much money.

And if you have already won all that money? Then the situation can now be discussed in the realm of possibility:

I just saw your story in the paper. What <u>will</u> you buy with a million dollars?

Going back to our opening question, then,

Standard: *If I were you* . . . This is standard usage because the verb form conveys something impossible (unless we are talking science fiction). Thus, you need the subjunctive *were*.

Non-standard: *If I was you* for many speakers is just fine, albeit non-standard. We certainly hear it in song lyrics. For example, Joan

The subjunctive: in the right mood

Osborn's "What If God Was One Of Us?" is joined by several other "I Wish I Was" titles and lyrics (do a search on lyrics.com).

A professional organization to which I belong sent a notice about their annual conference that included this line:

> *If you have a fee waiver for the basic registration fee (you would already know if this were the case), please register by February 10 to avoid late registration fees.*

Since it might well be the case that I have a fee waiver, the sentence didn't need to use a subjunctive *were*. However, the *if* in the first clause misled the writer into using a subjunctive verb form.

The subjunctive might be a thing of the past in a decade or two; currently, we can still make some semantic distinctions with this mood.

PRACTICE OPPORTUNITIES

Check to see if the verb forms in the following sentences are using the subjunctive in a standard way.

- *If you won the lottery, you will be rich.*
- *If I was you, I'd start the term paper tonight.*
- *If I was cooking dinner tonight, I'd make pasta.*
- *Lee is adamant that her best friend sits next to her.*

9

The passive (and active) structure: watch your voice

SOMETHING TO THINK ABOUT

Teachers always tell us to avoid the **passive** in writing. Why?

Question: Is passive the same as past tense?
Answer: No. A passive sentence can be in any tense.
Question: Why should the passive be avoided?
Answer: There is a bias against the passive form because it puts the doer of the action at the end of the sentence and thus seems to lack assertiveness. Active and passive sentences both have their uses.

The basics of the passive (and active) voice

My students very frequently think that a passive sentence is a sentence in the past tense. While that is not correct, I understand why they think so. Take this passive sentence:

The poodle is groomed by Monica.

82

The passive (and active) structure: watch your voice

The main verb is *groomed*, and it has that *–ed* ending. Here's another sentence in the passive:

The work is done by Monica.

Here, the main verb, *done*, is in its past participle form (third of the triplet *do/did/done*). In fact, both main verbs *groomed* and *done* are in the past participle, but *groomed* doesn't have a separate form from the simple past. The triplet is *groom/groomed/groomed*. Either way, these two sentences are passive. But passive what?

The passive is not a verb tense, even though it entails a change in the verb forms. It is a voice; these sentences are in the **passive voice**. The voices in English are active and passive, and the different voices are independent of tense, i.e. you can have either voice in the past, present, or future.

How do we passivize a sentence? We have to look at the passive's connection to the active voice. Look again at the passive sentence:

Passive: *The poodle is groomed by Monica.*

And see how it connects to its corresponding active version:

Active counterpart: *Monica grooms the poodle.*

A passive sentence is derived from a base form that is in the active voice. Notice that the active version above is in the present tense. Passivizing a sentence doesn't change its tense.

Here's how active sentences become passive. First, the subject and object switch places. So *the poodle* goes to the front of the sentence and *Monica* goes to the end. Then a "by-phrase" is created, in that the new object is the object of the preposition *by*: *by Monica*. Finally, the full verb is altered. A helping verb is created, and it has to be a form of *to be*.

The passive (and active) structure: watch your voice

Remember that helping verbs must convey time (as well as number and person) information, so the tense marker that has so far been on the main verb must jump onto the helping verb (this is actually called **tense jumping**), thus preserving the tense of the active sentence. Here *to be* as a helping verb becomes *is*, since the form *is* conveys the information of present tense, singular and third person, and the helping verb now agrees in number and person with the new subject, *the poodle*. What happens to the main verb? It is converted to its past participle form.

Here's a list of steps we took to get from the active to the passive form:

1   Subject and object change places.
2   Old subject is put into prepositional phrase (*by* + old subject).
3   *To be* helping verb is added (bare infinitive).
4   Tense of main verb jumps to helping verb *be*.
5   Helping verb agrees in person and number with the new subject.
6   Main verb converts to past participle form.

Figure 9.1 illustrates these conversion steps with a sentence that is in the past tense.

If the active sentence is in the past tense, then the full verb in the passive version will be as well: *Monica groomed the poodle → The poodle <u>was</u> groomed by Monica.*

1   *Monica* moves to the end of the sentence; add *by*, so prepositional phrase is *by Monica*.
2   *The poodle* moves to the front into the subject slot.
3   Helping verb *be* is added in front of the main verb.
4   Past tense marker jumps off *groomed* and onto helping verb *be*.
5   Helping verb agrees with new subject (third person singular) = *was*.
6   Main verb *groomed* converts to its past participle form = *groomed*.

Figure 9.1: Conversion of active to passive voice

The passive (and active) structure: watch your voice

Here are a few more active-to-passive conversions. Try mapping out the steps.

Wilma and Glen open a savings account → *A savings account is opened by Wilma and Glen.* (Present tense preserved; new subject is singular, so verb becomes singular *is*)

Liz hired additional help → *Additional help was hired by Liz.* (Past tense preserved)

What if the sentence already has a helping verb? We still need to insert *be* in the full verb.

Benny is watching the movie → *The movie is being watched by Benny.*

Here, our active sentence is in the present progressive. The present progressive-ness needs to be preserved when we passivize the sentence. The helping verb *be* is inserted between the existing helping verb and the main verb of the full verb. Now we have the construction *is + be + watching*. The inserted helping verb gets the *–ing* progressive marker of the main verb because of tense jumping. And the main verb? It turns into the past participle, *watched*.

Try another conversion:

Lori is completing this year's tax forms → *This year's tax forms are being completed by Lori.*

Notice here that the old *be* helping verb changed to the plural (*are*, not *is*) because it agrees with the new subject *tax forms*, not the old subject *Lori*. The new helping verb receives the progressive *–ing* ending, and the main verb converts to the past participle form.

The passive (and active) structure: watch your voice

Here's an active-to-passive conversion but with a verb that has a past participle form different from the simple past. Note also that the helping verb has to agree with the new subject:

Andy is writing the poems → The poems are being written by Andy.

Let's map out the conversion:

- *Andy* goes to the end of the sentence and is placed in a prepositional phrase.
- *The poems* goes to the front of the sentence.
- We add helping verb *be* between *is* and *writing*: *is + be + writing*.
- Now tense jumping: *be → being*.
- Main verb becomes past participle: *writing → written*.
- And *is*? It now must agree with the poems, so it becomes plural verb *are*.

All these insertions, jumps, etc. might seem very complicated, but we can passivize a sentence pretty quickly and without much thought. We (again) know a lot of these grammatical properties of our language intuitively.

Uses of the passive (and active) voice

Let's go back to all those teachers (and style guides) telling us to avoid the passive. In fact, my word-processing grammar checker is flagging all the passive sentences in this chapter and suggesting their active forms as better.

The passive (and active) structure: watch your voice

Is it that the passive has more words than the active? That the passive voice is somehow more confusing than the active? No, the answer is usually that a passive construction is considered "weak." The doer of the action is not up front in the subject slot. Sometimes we want the doer of the action in the subject slot, and thus we want the active voice.

The *doer*, by the way, is more officially called the **agent** of the sentence. Agent is a better term than subject when we discuss passives because even though the original subject of the active sentence becomes the object in the passive, it is still doing something. In

The poodle is groomed by Monica,

the grammatical subject is now the *poodle* – it's in the subject slot of the sentence – but *Monica* is still the doer, i.e. agent.

Sometimes we want to highlight the action or de-emphasize the agent. In an active sentence, the noun in the subject slot is in the spotlight. If I want the object in the spotlight, I can convert to a passive construction. So if *the poodle* is the focus of my sentence, not *Monica*, the passive sentence works better for my purposes. The same can be true of the movie that Benny is watching and the tax forms that Lori is completing.

The passive voice has its uses, and writers and speakers can choose it if it suits the job intended.

- Maybe I want to down-play the agent of the action:

  That cat is so pampered by its owner

  (where I want the cat in the spotlight, i.e. in the front of the sentence).

- Maybe I want to leave out the agent altogether:

  The lamp was broken in the middle of the night

  (and I don't want to say who did it).

The passive (and active) structure: watch your voice

- Maybe I don't know the agent:

  The car was vandalized.

Look at this sentence:

The secret was revealed.

Here, there is no agent mentioned at all. The active version would be:

Someone revealed the secret.

But if I don't want to accuse anyone, or don't know who the agent is, it's better to go with the passive construction. Similarly, with a sentence like

The car was stolen,

I could say:

Someone stole the car,

but in reality the noun in the spotlight is the missing car, and the passive serves my purpose better. These specific passives are called **agentless passives** (some books call them "truncated passives"). As you see, they have their uses too.

Another reason someone might prefer the passive voice has to do with the known/new pattern of information. I tell you:

Hank opened a bank account.

You now know about Hank and the bank account. I now want to add information about the bank account, so the older information moves to the front and my new information goes at the end of the sentence for emphasis:

The passive (and active) structure: watch your voice

The bank account was later closed by Hank's brother.

I wound up with a passive sentence since *bank account* can't be an agent.

So both active and passive constructions have their uses. The problem is that writers tend to use the passive in places where the active gives a clearer meaning (I am not sure why; maybe it sounds more formal). A colleague of mine who teaches freshman writing has coined the abbreviation TDP for The Dreaded Passive. She can't stand the sight of TDP anymore, and her students know that points will be deducted for veering into the passive voice. I resist all-out war on passives; my message instead is to be mindful of which sentence construction you use.

A few more words about the passive. In Chapter 2, we saw that stative verbs don't passivize.

Miriam senses a problem

is an example of a verb conveying a state of being.

*A problem is sensed by Miriam

doesn't work.

Judy feels sorry for the stray dog

also uses a stative verb, so we can't passivize:

*The stray dog is felt sorry for by Judy.

Sentences with object complements can be converted into the passive voice:

Jerry appoints the shy student attendance monitor/The shy student is appointed attendance monitor by Jerry.

The passive (and active) structure: watch your voice

Sentences with subject complements, however, cannot:

Allen is a mathematician/*A mathematician is been by Allen.

(Remember * indicates a structure that isn't well formed in any dialect.)

Chapter 6 has more on complements.

Finally, sometimes we see passive constructions that employ the helping verb *to get* instead of *to be*: for example,

We got robbed!

This construction is considered an **informal passive**. It's not standard, but it works in informal situations.

PRACTICE OPPORTUNITIES

Passivize the following sentences and identify the tense of the active versions:

- *Anin has tutored Mayra once a week all term.*
- *Karina is reading the new best-seller.*

Put the following sentences back into their active forms:

- *Adam was spotted by his fans.*
- *Zena has been being observed by her boss.*

10

The case of pronouns

What's the difference among I, me, and myself?

Question: Is it *Jasvinda and I* or *Jasvinda and me*?
Answer: You can't tell from this phrase alone. If Jasvinda and I are doing something, i.e. are the subjects, then it is *Jasvinda and I*, but it's *Jasvinda and me* if we two are the objects of the sentence. So *Jasvinda and I sat on the terrace*, but *It was too noisy for Jasvinda and me to talk* – and *Joanna saw Jasvinda and me go inside*.
Question: When do you use *whom*?
Answer: *Whom* is the object form of *who*, so use *whom* when it is not in the subject slot of the sentence.

The basics of pronouns

Going back to your elementary school memories, you can probably recall the statement, "A pronoun takes the place of a noun." True, and of course not that simple. In general, **pronouns** do stand in for nouns. The noun that gives the pronoun meaning is called the **antecedent** (notice the *ante*, as in *come before*). The antecedent does not literally need to come first in a sentence, but it must give the pronoun meaning.

The case of pronouns

Pronouns are tricky, for a couple of reasons. First, a pronoun must agree with its antecedent in number, person, and gender. English doesn't have much gender differentiation, but we do in the pronoun system, at least in the third person (*he* vs. *she* vs. *it*).

Second, pronouns must convey the **case** of their own role in the sentence. Case signals the role being performed by the word, e.g. subject of the sentence, object, etc. Pronouns, then, change their form depending on their grammatical function in a sentence. So a pronoun in the subject slot of a sentence (*I, he, she*) has a form different from that pronoun if it moves to the object slot (*me, him, her*).

If the pronoun is in the subject slot of the sentence, it must be in the **nominative case**. A pronoun in the object slot will be in the **objective case**. A pronoun in a sentence reflecting an entity that possesses something is in the **possessive case** (also called the genitive case).

In the sentence

She saw us when he lowered his newspaper,

she and *he* are in the nominative case (subjects of the two clauses); *us* is in the objective case (signaling its role as direct object); and *his* is in the possessive case.

(English actually can be analyzed as having more cases. For example, some linguists see indirect objects as being in the dative case. Since direct and indirect object pronouns have the same form, though, we can say they both take the objective case.)

Chapter 6 has more on objects.

When we choose a pronoun, then, there is a good deal of calculation involved (and various opportunities for non-standard matching of antecedent and pronoun). Often, this calculating is done automatically: we dip into our linguistic competence. But sometimes we hesitate: is it *I* or *me*?

In addition, not all English dialects use pronouns the same way, so we probably hear sentences like *Him and me went to the store* (where an objective case pronoun is in the subject slot) or *The professor is sending Ralph and I to the office* (where a nominative case pronoun is in an object slot).

Thus, pronouns can cause problems for English users. Further, we are aware that there are problems. In other words, we surely have been told by people in authority, "It's I, not me"; and have heard grammarians railing against improper use of pronouns. Hence, all of us have most likely asked or been asked the questions that started off this chapter (I certainly have).

Here's another pronoun situation that causes people to hesitate:

Tony loves tennis better than____. Is it *I* or *me*?

If you put *I* in the slot (nominative case), you mean that

Tony loves tennis better than I (do).

Here, the word *than* is used as a conjunction, followed by *I do* (but with implied verb). This is more standard than choosing *me*.

By putting *me* in the slot (objective case), *tennis* and *me* are both entities Tony likes, but he likes the sport better. Here, the word *than* is the preposition for the prepositional phrase *than me*.

Chapter 12 has more on prepositions.

Chapter 13 has more on conjunctions.

If the context doesn't clarify what is being compared, be mindful of which pronoun you use.

This chapter is about pronouns, and there are lots of subtypes, which I list in Table 10.1.

Table 10.1: All pronoun types

Personal
Reflexive
Indefinite/universal
Demonstrative
Reciprocal
Interrogative
Relative

Uses of personal pronouns

We'll go through each type here; other chapters in this text give further information about several of these pronoun categories. Let's start with **personal pronouns**. In Chapter 2, we saw all of the possible subjects for all the possible sentences of English, divided by number (singular/plural) and person (first, second, third). To review, first person means the speaker. If in the plural, *we*, the pronoun reflects the speaker and those whom the speaker is including in his or her statement. (Notice that *we* is a bit ambiguous. It can mean the speaker and the listener or the speaker and someone else not present. *Remember when we went to Vegas?* could refer to a trip that either did or didn't include the listener(s).)

Second person means the listener. Third person means another party, neither the speaker nor the listener. The third person singular must accurately reflect the antecedent's gender, *he* or *she*, and even whether the antecedent is animate or not, *he/she* vs. *it*. (Speakers may differ in their use of *it*. Some people refer to boats as *she*, for example, or cats as *she* and dogs as *he*, whereas others call unspecified animals *it*.)

Let's try some examples of converting nouns to pronouns:

> *Awilda voted in Awilda's first election. Awilda's family was proud of Awilda and threw Awilda a party to celebrate. The greatest sense of pride was Awilda's.*

So many *Awildas*! If we turn these nouns into pronouns, they all have to be third person singular and feminine. The possessive *Awilda's* will become either *her* or *hers*. (We'll keep the first noun a noun to establish identity.)

> *Awilda voted in her first election. Her family was proud of her and threw her a party to celebrate. The greatest sense of pride was hers.*

Table 10.2 lists all the personal pronouns by case.

Table 10.2: Personal pronouns by case

Nominative case	Objective case	Possessive case
I	me	my/mine
you	you	your/yours
he	him	his/his
she	her	her/hers
it	it	its/its
we	us	our/ours
you (pl.)	you (pl.)	your/yours (pl.)
they	them	their/theirs

Note that in the possessive, there are two forms. A possessive pronoun like *her* doesn't take the place of the noun; it takes the place of the possessor and modifies what is being owned (*Shari's car → Her car*). *Hers*, however, takes the place of both the possessor and what is being possessed (*Shari's car → hers*). The former is called an **adjectival possessive pronoun**; the latter is a **nominal possessive pronoun**.

Do you notice, by the way, that all the nominal possessive pronouns end in *–s* except for *mine*? This irregularity of Standard English has been regularized in some dialects of English, so that some speakers use *mines*: *That house is mines*. While this is a stigmatized form, understanding the patterns, and exceptions, of the pronoun forms helps us understand why they exist. (We will see more irregularity in reflexive pronouns, later.)

Now we can answer the question that opened this chapter: is it *Jasvinda and I* or *Jasvinda and me*? It depends. What job is this phrase doing in the larger sentence? If the two people are the subjects of the sentence, then *Jasvinda and I* works. If they are objects, then we want *Jasvinda and me*. The objective case, remember, works for both direct and indirect objects. It would also be the case for objects of prepositions.

The following structures, then, would be standard:

Jasvinda and I took our driving tests. (Pronoun is subject)

The driving teacher passed Jasvinda and me. (Pronoun is direct object)

The Motor Vehicles Bureau mailed Jasvinda and me our results. (Pronoun is indirect object)

The driving teacher shook hands with Jasvinda and me. (Pronoun is object of preposition *with*)

(Notice that *Jasvinda* never changes form in the sentences above, even though the noun is placed in various slots. In the case of nouns, case marking is not overt unless we talk about *Jasvinda's car.*)

The case of pronouns

Choosing between the nominative pronoun *I* and the objective case *me* can be anxiety-producing for some speakers. Since we probably have echoes of "it's I, not me" in our heads, many speakers adopt a strategy whereby they avoid *me* altogether and just go with *I*, as in the prepositional phrase *between you and I*. Given that this is a prepositional phrase, the pronouns should be in the objective case to be standard (*you* is the same form in both cases, so the second person pronoun is not affected). Many very educated, learned, grammatical speakers, however, are comfortable with the wording *between you and I*. In fact, some linguists defend this structure. Others call it hypercorrection and a result of insecurity.

Others solve the *I* vs. *me* conflict by choosing *me*. I found the following sentence in *The New York Times* (August 2, 2009, page 8): "She Asks About Love But Sure Isn't Telling" by Dave Itzkoff. Charlyne Yi says, "Whether or not me and Michael are together or were ever together is irrelevant."

There is a song by the Scottish group Belle and Sebastian called "Me and the Major" (with "Me and the Major" in the subject slot in the lyrics). So in conversation, in song lyrics, etc. we see variation on the standard use of pronouns.

Here are some more non-standard varieties of personal pronouns:

She loves shoes, my friend.

She is what's called a "redundant pronoun." It is found in some non-standard dialects.

Related to redundancy is "topicalization":

My friend, she loves shoes.

Topicalization plants the antecedent at the start of the sentence and then follows with the related pronoun.

Uses of reflexive pronouns

Another strategy I have noticed employed when people are shy about the *I* vs. *me* distinction is to use a more neutral (and perhaps educated-sounding) *myself*: *If you have any questions, do not hesitate to get in contact with Ms. Jones or myself.*

Myself is a type of pronoun called a **reflexive pronoun** (see Table 0 in the Cheat Sheet at the back of the book) and is used to reinforce a statement, such as

I, myself, solved the puzzle.

It is also used when the antecedent is nearby, as in

Jill saw herself on television.

Jill saw her on television wouldn't mean the same thing.

The tangle we can get into with *myself* is parodied in the 1997 film *Austin Powers: International Man of Mystery*, when Mike Myers, as the (somewhat pompous) title character, says to a new acquaintance, "Allow myself to introduce myself." Even Mr. Powers hesitates before that second *myself*, knowing something is awry.

The reflexive pronouns follow the number and person pattern of the personal pronouns. In addition, the singular reflexives take the suffix *–self* and the plurals take *–selves*. Can you figure out from Cheat Sheet Table 0 what stem is used? Most reflexives are formed by taking the adjectival possessive pronoun and adding *–self* or *–selves*. So the formula gives us *my + self, our + selves*, etc.

There are two exceptions, however. Given the formula I just stated, the third person singular masculine form should be *his + self*

= *hisself*, and the third person plural form should be *their* + *selves* = *theirselves*. These two forms, however, take the objective case pronoun as the stem (*himself* and *themselves*). Here is another instance in which the Standard English form is not necessarily the most regular. Further, forms that smooth out the irregularity and use *hisself* and *theirselves* (or *theirself*, since some dialects don't pluralize the suffix) tend to be stigmatized, seen as wrong and uneducated. They are non-standard, for sure, but in a way this system is less messy than the irregular forms of Standard English.

So far we have seen personal pronouns (subcategorized by case as nominative, object, and two types of possessive) and reflexive pronouns. We still have other types of pronouns to discuss.

Uses of other pronoun types

Indefinite pronouns

Indefinite pronouns were mentioned in Chapter 4 when we discussed problems of subject–verb agreement.

Everyone should pick up his or her paper

includes the singular pronoun *everyone* that (in a way) means a bunch of people. We don't actually specify who *everyone* is, so we call these types of pronouns **indefinite pronouns** (some books call them universal, but I will go with indefinite as the category name).

Someone forgot to pick up his or her paper,

similarly, has a pronoun in the subject slot (*someone*) that refers to an unnamed person; hence, it is also an indefinite pronoun.

Now take the sentence

Someone forgot to pick up their paper.

Someone is a singular antecedent to plural pronoun *their*, leading to a mismatch. But do we have a gender neutral pronoun we can use instead? Guidebooks tell us to use *his or her*:

Someone forgot to pick up his or her paper.

That construction seems cumbersome to many of us, who just go with plural *their*.

Other indefinite pronouns include the *A MAN'S* words from Chapter 4 (*all, most, any, none, some*) and the words formed with the suffix *–one*, *–body*, or *–thing*.

Demonstrative pronouns

We saw demonstrative pronouns in Chapter 5 as part of the regular determiners. These words are *this*, *that*, *these*, and *those*. They point to (demonstrate) an entity or activity.

Reciprocal pronouns

These pronouns include *each other* and *one another*. Did you know they have different meanings? *Each other* refers to two entities. *One another* refers to three or more entities.

The twins were talking with each other; the triplets were talking with one another.

Interrogative pronouns

The interrogative pronouns are w*ho, whom, whose*, and *what.*

These wh-words show up at the beginning of what are called **wh-interrogatives** or information questions (the answer to the question requires information).

Note the distinction between

Who is at the door?

and

With whom are you meeting?

The first sentence uses *who* as the subject = nominative case. The second sentence uses *whom* as the object of the preposition = objective case. (More on *who/whom* below.)

Relative pronouns

We just saw *who* and *whom* as interrogative pronouns. These words can also function in a different capacity. *Who* and *whom* are two of a handful of relative pronouns in English, those words that derive from an antecedent in the main sentence, reduced to a pronoun form in a dependent clause called the **relative clause**. The full list is *who, whom, whose, which*, and *that.*

Chapter 14 has more on relative pronouns and relative clauses.

To illustrate the overlap in the interrogative and relative pronoun categories, I give you:

<u>*Who*</u> *is at the door?*

and

> *The author <u>who</u> wrote the novel lives in Scotland.*

The first *who* is an interrogative pronoun; the second is a relative pronoun.

Who vs. *whom*

Be it with interrogative or relative pronouns, the *who/whom* distinction confuses people. *Who* is in the nominative case and *whom* is in the objective case. The distinction is the same as the *I/me* difference. For many speakers, *whom* is fading from usage (*who* doing double duty), except in set phrases such as *to whom it may concern*. (In fact, when I typed *to whom*, my computer automatically suggested the full phrase.)

> *Who did Walt go to the movies with last night?*

sounds perfectly fine to most of us. Chapter 12 will discuss the rule that prepositions shouldn't be placed at the end of a sentence, separated from their objects. If we wanted to follow the rule against ending with prepositions, we'd get the construction

> *With who did Walt go to the movies last night?*

and most of us would then switch to *whom*. Actually, some English speakers would be most comfortable saying the *who . . . with* version but writing the *with whom* version.

If you are not too secure in your abilities to discern nominative from objective case, there is a rule of thumb that works most of the time. When you are choosing between *who* and *whom*, look at the following word. If it's a verb, you probably want *who* since it will function as the subject of that verb. If the following word is a noun, you probably want *whom* since the subject is most likely already in the sentence.

Let's try some:

Nan reads authors who/whom tackle social issues. (*who* = subject of relative clause, paired with predicate *tackle social issues*)

Mel knows the teacher who/whom the principal promoted. (*whom* = direct object of *promoted*)

And this is where the rule of thumb doesn't work:

Who/m did Peter text during class?

The standard form is *whom*, even though the following word is a verb; that's because the following word is a helping verb. *Whom* is the object. If you turn the sentence into its declarative form, it will be clearer:

Peter texted <u>whom</u> during class.

I always tell my students that if they aren't too sure which to use, it's better to go with *who*. A misuse of *who* (where in standard form it should be *whom*) is less noticeable than the other way around. But just as the pronoun *I* seems to be elevated in prestige due to all those adults correcting us, some English users believe *whom* is more correct somehow, regardless of its sentence position. Thus we find hypercorrections of *whom*, as in

He is a man whom will save the planet

(seriously! – in some ad I came across), and on a t-shirt I saw at my gym:

I root for whomever beats Harvard.

The case of pronouns

This last sentence is non-standard because the wh-word is the subject of the predicate *beats Harvard*. The t-shirt maker (and wearer too, I guess) misidentified the wh-word as the object of the preposition *for* (the whole second clause is the object of the preposition); and they probably had a leaning for the more educated-sounding *whom*.

Table P (see Cheat Sheet at the back of the book) offers a brief rule-of-thumb guide on the distinction between *who* and *whom*.

The case after *to be*

I remember in 2nd grade practicing telephone etiquette. Each of us was called to the (unplugged) phone on the teacher's desk and pretended to answer. The teacher would ask, "Is X there?" (and insert our name). And we were to reply, "This is she (or he)." I probably never in my life answered the phone that way again. Here's another example of an adult telling kids that the nominative case *I* is somehow better than the objective form *me*.

But why is "This is she" more standard? In Chapter 4, we saw that some words occur in the subject slot of a sentence but are just placeholders; they are called dummy subjects. So in *This is she*, the word *this* is a dummy subject. The real subject has to be in the nominative case, *she*. Take the sentence

The winner was he,

and remember *to be* is a linking verb. I likened linking verbs (in Chapter 2) to equals signs, so we could rewrite this sentence as

The winner = he.

The rule here is that the copula verb *to be* does not take a direct object. The material in the predicate (following *to be*) is the complement (discussed in Chapter 6). The case on both sides of the verb would be the same: nominative = nominative. English doesn't have case markings on nouns, so *This is Susan* doesn't ask speakers to choose a case; *This is* ___ (*she/her*) does.

Vague pronouns

Here's a final note mainly about written English. You might have had teachers identify in your writing what is termed a **vague pronoun**. The pronoun's antecedent should be clear to the reader. Take a sentence like the following: *Sally and Anne went to pick up her car.* Who is *her*? It might be clear from the context, but the writer needs to make sure.

Here's another example of a vague pronoun:

In Sylvia Plath's poem "Sheep in Fog," she makes effective use of metaphor.

Who is *she*? It is logical that the writer means Sylvia Plath, but that proper noun is not actually stated, just its possessive form. Picky teachers (I admit to being one) would probably ask students to reword that sentence, maybe to something like *Sylvia Plath makes effective use of metaphor in the poem "Sheep in Fog,"* where there is no need for a pronoun at all.

A final example of vague pronouns is over-use of the word "this." Take the sentences,

Sylvia Plath lived in England during the coldest winter in decades. She was also separated from her husband and raising two small children. This contributed to her depression.

What is the antecedent of *this*? It's unclear.

PRACTICE OPPORTUNITIES

Evaluate the use of pronouns in these sentences:

- *The results were positive for Barbara and I.*
- *If it's me they want, that's who they'll get.*
- *Did you hear who Andrea bought tickets from? She's an old elementary school pal of mine who I haven't seen in years.*

11

Adjectives and adverbs modifying

When someone says, "How are you?" what do you normally answer? Do you think your answer is grammatical?

Question: Is it *I feel <u>bad</u>* or *I feel <u>badly</u>*?
Answer: *I feel <u>bad</u>* if you are talking about an inner state.
Question: Is it *I am good* or *I am well*?
Answer: "I am well" is the answer to give if you are being asked about your physical and emotional state (which you probably are). "I am good" relates more broadly to include moral and ethical status, as in "She's a good person." However, "I'm good" as an answer to "How are you?" is becoming commonplace.

The basics of adjectives and adverbs

Adjectives and **adverbs** are parts of speech that modify. They each work in separate territories. Adjectives modify nouns and pronouns, and adverbs modify verbs. However, adverbs can also modify adjectives and other adverbs. (See Table Q in the Cheat Sheet at the back of the book for a summary of functions.) Why are these two word types discussed in the same chapter? They often look alike: adverbs usually – but not always – are the adjective form with the –*ly* ending:

Slow = adjective
Slowly = adverb

Further, there is dialectal variation in usage, so that some choose adjectives when standard grammar calls for adverbs, and vice versa. Let's take *slow* and *slowly*.

Derrick is slow. He walks slowly.

The adjective *slow* modifies the noun *Derrick*. The adverb *slowly* modifies the walking he does, i.e. the verb. Using *slowly* is the standard way to discuss Derrick's languid movement, but it probably sounds fine to some to say

Derrick walks slow

or

He walks too slow or *very slow.*

Remember that not all adverbs take the –*ly* ending. So contrasting Derrick, above, to Denise, we can say that

Denise is fast

and

She walks fast, not *fastly!*

Fast in the second sentence is an adverb since it modifies how the action is being done. However, it doesn't take the –*ly* ending. These adverbs without –*ly* endings are called "flat adverbs."

Uses of adjectives and adverbs

The opening distinction about *feel bad* vs. *badly* will become clearer if we think back to the concept of linking verbs. *To feel* has two meanings, one linking a subject to a description of the subject's state, and one to the action of using fingertips. If my fingertips are numb and I can't feel anything with them, I am *feeling badly*. It's more likely that I'm telling you something about the subject (me). Remember that linking verbs can be thought of as equals signs, so *I feel bad* can be mapped out as *I = bad*. Here, the modifying word is an adjective modifying the subject.

> *I feel badly* = poor sense of touch
> *I feel bad* = disturbed inner state

The "correct" answer to our first question, then, is that when our inner state isn't in the best shape, we are *feeling bad*. It could well be that the over-use of the adverb *badly* here is compensation for all those times children were corrected by adults in situations where they used an adjective and the standard form was an adverb. I often hear

> *I feel badly,*

however, when people express regret. So is it "wrong"? It's non-standard but perhaps taking over as the more common form.

Do we ever use *badly*, though? Yes, in cases where an action isn't executed in an excellent manner, as in

> *I play tennis badly.*

The question about adjectives vs. adverbs continues with *good* vs. *well*. In general, *good* is an adjective and *well* is an adverb. So you can do a *good job* and *play the clarinet well*. The problem is that *well* can also be an adjective when it relates to someone's health or emotional state (well-being). If you are not feeling *bad*, you're feeling *well*. (There is a temptation to employ *good* since it is such a natural antonym of bad.) So

I am well

has that linking verb construction of

I = well.

Saying someone is good (*George is a good person*) means that person is kind and decent. Think of *good* related to *goodness*; *well* related to *wellness* and *well-being*.

No one really minds if you answer the query, "How are you?" with "Good." But if you are reading this chapter, you are curious about the distinction. Some people answer "Fine" or even "How are you?" And if you really think about it, this greeting is more a ritual than a genuine query, anyway.

Verb forms as adjectives

English allows the present and past participle verb forms to be used as adjectives. When used in this way, these main verbs appear without their helping verbs.

Chapters 2 and 3 have more on verb forms.

Present participle as adjective

Take a sentence we encountered in Chapter 5:

Running water calms Sid down.

Present participle as part of progressive verb form

In contrast, if I said

The water is running,

then *running* would be the main verb of the full verb *is running*, conveying the present progressive tense. Contrast this to the Sid sentence above, where *running* modifies the noun *water* and is an adjective.

Past participle as adjective

The past participle can also occur without a helping verb, not acting as a verb, but in this case modifying a noun:

The frozen lake looked beautiful.

Past participle as part of perfect verb form

Compare the sentence above with

The lake has frozen over,

where *frozen* is the main verb of the full verb *has frozen*, conveying the present perfect tense. In *The frozen lake*, the past participle modifies the noun *lake*.

Past participle as part of passive voice

In the sentence

The vegetables were frozen,

however, the word *frozen* could be ambiguous. It looks like it's in the full verb of the passive voice (helping verb = *to be*, main verb = past participle). But the meaning of the sentence is probably not

The vegetables were frozen by someone.

The past participle here is more likely an adjective, along the lines of

The vegetables were green.

If we say

The vegetables were eaten,

then we have the passive voice (. . . *were eaten by someone*).

> *Chapter 9 has more on passive sentences.*

Adverbs modifying adjectives and other adverbs

Adjectives modify two parts of speech: nouns (*the lenient teacher*) and pronouns (*she is lenient*). Adverbs modify three separate parts of speech: verbs, other adverbs, and adjectives.

We have seen someone *walk slowly* (adverb modifying verb). How slowly? *Very slowly.* *Very* is an adverb modifying the other adverb *slowly*. And how lenient is the teacher? *Incredibly lenient.* *Incredibly* is the adverb modifying the adjective *lenient*.

Placement of adverbs

Usually, the modifying word is placed close to the word it modifies. Adjectives have some freedom to move about, so we can have *the red ball* and *the ball is red*; as well as *it is red*, but not **the red it*.

Adverbs have even more freedom of movement. We could say

Tim <u>nervously</u> started the car, or
<u>*Nervously*</u>, *Tim started the car*, or maybe even
Tim started the car <u>nervously</u>.

There is some limitation, however. Note that we can't say

*Tim started nervously the car.

English doesn't allow the adverb to come between the main verb and the direct object.

Usage books in general advise placing adverbs as close to their modifying words as possible. There are some adverbs, though, that modify the whole sentence. They are called **sentential adverbs**.

Let's look at this sentence:

Hopefully, it won't rain on Saturday.

What word is *hopefully* modifying? None, really. It's more that the entire statement is being uttered (or written) with hope. Some grammarians don't approve of this use of *hopefully* as a sentential adverb. They believe that we could say

Hopefully, Tim checked his grades on-line (he checked with hope),

but not our *raining* sentence. In real usage, though, sentential adverbs exist, and *hopefully* is one.

Some other examples of sentential adverbs include:

Amazingly, the rain stopped just as we got to the park.

The adverb is modifying the whole statement, not any one word.

Interestingly, Henry Hudson was working for the Dutch when he sailed into New York Harbor.

There is no one word that *interestingly* modifies; it is the fact being conveyed in the full sentence that is of interest.

Comparative and superlative adjectives and adverbs

Adjectives and adverbs also have the power to compare two or more objects and actions. Derrick and Denise, above, can be compared this way:

Derrick is slow. He is slower than Denise. He is the slowest person I know.

Denise is fast. She is faster than Derrick. She is the fastest person I know.

Here, the adjectives *slow* and *fast* are put through their paces, and we see them in their **comparative** *-er* forms when comparing two entities; and in their **superlative** *-est* forms when the comparison is among more than two people or objects.

In general, when an adjective is longer than two syllables, the *-er* and *-est* suffixes would make the word too long, and we use an alternate way to form the comparative and superlative. We don't use suffixes but instead the words *more* and *the most*, *less* and *the least*. Take the adjective *studious*:

> Sienna is studious. She is <u>more studious</u> than Myles. She is <u>the most studious</u> pupil in the class.

> Myles is not too studious. He is <u>less studious</u> than Sienna. He is <u>the least studious</u> pupil in the class (but he is trying hard!).

There are some short adjectives that are a bit ambiguous. Back in Chapter 3, I wrote *more subtle* in a sentence, and my grammar checker flagged it and suggested instead *subtler*, which sounds awkward to me.

Adverbs also have comparative and superlative forms, and (yes) sometimes these forms are replaced by their adjectival counterparts.

> Luis digs deeply into the mystery. He digs more deeply every day. He digs the most deeply as the grant money runs out.

Note that, because the adverb *deeply* has a suffix, the comparative/ superlative forms use the separate words *more* and *the most*. Consider

> He digs the most deeply.

While that is standard, most people would say

> He digs deeper every day and deeper yet as the money runs out.

Conjunctive adverbs

Another type of adverb is called a **conjunctive adverb**. It is easily confused with conjunctions.

Chapter 13 has more on conjunctions.

Take the word *however*. The most common run-on sentence is created when writers treat *however* as a conjunction, as in

Howard and Myrna went to Cape Cod, however, they forgot their swimsuits.

However doesn't qualify as a conjunction between these two clauses, and thus the comma before *however* is too weak. We need a stronger punctuation mark such as a period or semi-colon. Thus, we can fix the punctuation in a few ways:

. . . Cape Cod; however, . . . and
. . . Cape Cod. However, . . .

Chapter 16 has more on semi-colons.

Table 11.1 lists several common conjunctive adverbs. Notice that these words do link thoughts together, but they aren't punctuated the way conjunctions are.

As you go about your reading and writing in the next week, try to notice such words and the punctuation marks that surround them.

Chapter 16 has more on punctuation.

Table 11.1: Common conjunctive adverbs

Consequently
Furthermore
However
Meanwhile
Moreover
Nevertheless
Thus

Note that adjectives and adverbs can act as modifiers even when they are part of a larger unit, either a phrase or a clause.

Chapter 14 has more on adjective and adverb phrases and clauses.

Negation

Many grammarians call the words used to negate sentences (*no*, *not*, *never*, etc.) adverbs. So let's talk about them in this chapter. The question I didn't even need to pose in my initial list of questions was, "What's wrong with double negatives?" No one asks me that; everyone "knows" what's wrong: two negatives make a positive, so double negatives are illogical.

There are a few things wrong with that logic. First, not all double negatives cancel each other out:

It is not without regret that I must fire you.

This example is grammatical in Standard English. In fact, it might sound downright formal. But there are two negative words in it (*not* and *without*). In this case, of course, the speaker ultimately means the positive (well, as positive as you can get having to tell someone, *You're fired*). The two negatives temper the meaning; the speaker is not gleeful about what he or she has to do. The two negatives, thus, work together and express a different meaning from a corresponding sentence without any negatives.

Here's another example of a double negative that you won't think is illogical:

We can't not bring a gift

(especially when spoken with emphasis on *not*). The meaning here is a bit different from

We can/will bring a gift.

What about when two negatives work to emphasize the negative?

Carole is never going to have nothing to do with Allard again.

The meaning is clearly that this relationship is a dud, and the force of the statement comes across clearly as well. The speaker or writer used a double negative construction (yes, non-standard), but we get the message. The bottom line: sometimes double negatives are logical, but be mindful of your use of them nonetheless.

PRACTICE OPPORTUNITIES

Identify the adjectives and adverbs in the following sentences and explain what they modify. Convert any non-standard forms to the standard.

* *Don't speak too loud in the office.*
* *Rosemary is a very speedy typist.*

- *She writes worse than a pre-schooler.*
- *Her penmanship is worse than a doctor's.*
- *She types well, however.*
- *I am well.*
- *I'm good.*

Apple has the slogan "Think Different." Is this grammatical?

12

Prepositional phrases and verb particles

Discuss the use of the word "up" in the following sentences:

Turn up the street. Turn up the heat.

Is "up" being used in the same way?

Question: Can you end a sentence with a **preposition**?
Answer: Strict grammarians still frown upon such a structure. Sometimes, however, it is more cumbersome to try to avoid it.

The basics of prepositional phrases

A **phrase** is a group of words without a subject–verb pair. Thus, a phrase doesn't have the status of a complete sentence. We've read so far about prepositional phrases. Here we'll talk some more about prepositions, the prepositional phrase, and a two-part verb that often looks like a verb + preposition, but isn't, called a **phrasal verb**.

My 5th grade teacher said that a **preposition** describes anything a cat can do in a parking lot (it's the silly stuff we remember). Where is the cat? *Under* the car, *in front of* the car, *behind* the car, *next to* the car, etc. These are location prepositions (also called locative). Notice that some prepositions are single words and some are phrases, and that prepositions are always followed by an object (noun or pronoun and any modifying material that goes with it). In these examples, *car* is the object of the preposition. (We can also say it is the object in the prepositional phrase.) The whole package, preposition + object = prepositional phrase. And if the object is a pronoun, it is put into the objective case: *next to Nancy* → *next to her* (not *she*). (Of course with possessive nouns and pronouns, we get possessive cases, as in *next to Nancy's desk* → *next to hers*.)

> Chapter 6 has more on objects.
>
> Chapter 10 has more on pronoun case.

Prepositions also convey information about time. When was the cat in the parking lot? *During* the night, *between* 12 and 2, *over* the weekend, *in* the morning. These prepositions are time prepositions (also called temporal). Again, they are followed by a noun or pronoun, together making up the prepositional phrase.

So far prepositions seem relatively concrete. What about the prepositional phrase *by Shakespeare*, though? The preposition *by* doesn't convey location or time information. It is, instead, a metaphorical preposition (some books use the term idiomatic preposition). Others of this type are found in the sentences

I have concerns about the environment

and

There's a report on TV (nothing is literally *on* the TV, except maybe a cable box).

Uses of prepositional phrases

Sometimes the object of the preposition moves around in the sentence, so we have sentences like *Who did you give a present to?* The prepositional phrase is *to who(m)*.

> *Chapter 10 has more on who vs. whom.*

Of course we could keep the full prepositional phrase together and say

To whom did you give a present?

but that sounds a bit formal. English grammar was codified by scholars who believed Latin had the ultimate, exemplary grammar. Latin conveys some types of information in noun forms that English would convey instead in preposition choice. Thus, we can't separate the prepositional information from its object in Latin; English is a different story.

Strict grammarians still say we should keep the prepositional phrase intact. Sometimes, though, it's actually quite cumbersome to avoid ending in a preposition. You might have heard Winston Churchill's parody about the restriction on sentence-final pre-positions:

It is something up with which I will not put.

(Others say it was not uttered by Churchill.) If you are concerned about a reader's reaction, try to keep the prepositional phrase together in professional writing.

In a new(ish) usage in English, some prepositions occur without objects altogether:

Prepositional phrases and verb particles

Wanna come with?

The object *me* or *us* is implied. English is also experiencing a change in the use of metaphorical prepositions. My colleague Cindy Mercer and I have written about college students using such expressions as

The movie is based off of the book,

where Cindy and I (a lot older than our students) would say or write *based on*. We also recently heard on the radio

I was afraid from my life,

another idiomatic change.

There is regional variation in preposition use as well. New York City residents tend to wait *on* line when the rest of the country waits *in* line. And sometimes prepositions double up (flagged as ungrammatical by style books), as in

Get off of the elevator at reception (vs. *get off the elevator*).

Standard British would use

She is in hospital, and *at university.*

Chicano English would use the construction

We're on 12th grade.

A French friend, whose English is pretty good, imports one of her native language prepositions when she says

I am allergic from cats.

Indian Standard English has the usage

Pay attention on your studies.

And several English dialects use an extra preposition (and leave out the verb) in

Where you at?

Keep an eye open for prepositional changes in the next five years; the prepositional system is in flux.

The basics of verb particles

Let's return to the sentences that started the chapter:

Turn up the street vs. *Turn up the heat.*

The word *up* in each sentence has a different grammatical role. In which sentence is it a preposition? In the first. *Up the street* is a prepositional phrase. What about in the second sentence? The whole verb is *turn up*. This is a two-part verb, called a **phrasal verb**, and the second part, resembling a preposition, is called a **verb particle**.

Other two-part verbs include *turn on, turn in, follow up, load up, give up, pick up, take off, tear off, put away, cross out,* and *write down.* And we can't forget the phrasal verbs that epitomized a certain 1960s subculture: *tune in, turn on,* and *drop out.* Nouns that follow these phrasal verbs, e.g. *write down <u>the phone number</u>*, are direct objects, not objects of a preposition.

Chapter 6 has more on objects.

Uses of verb particles

The *up's* in the two sentences above not only play different roles in the sentences; they also behave differently. A verb particle can move away from its verb to the end of the sentence after the object, so

Turn up the heat

can become

Turn the heat up.

This action is called **particle movement**. It is a property of phrasal verbs, but only ones with direct objects following, i.e. transitive verbs. A sentence with an intransitive phrasal verb won't see movement:

The grammar craze will never <u>die off</u>.

Chapter 7 has more on verb transitivity.

In contrast, a preposition can't move around a lot.

Turn up the street

cannot become

*Turn the street up.

Prepositional phrases and verb particles

If you are following standard grammar and avoiding the sentence-final preposition, you might still get a particle at the end of a sentence:

Please turn the heat up

and

Did the lights turn on?

Finally, prepositions might create ambiguity if we don't pay attention. Take

Martha drove her car from Detroit to Indiana.

Did she drive from Detroit to Indiana or just to Indiana and the car was manufactured in Detroit? The sentence might not be ambiguous in context, but we could also say

Martha drove the car manufactured in Detroit to Indiana.

Don't overlook those little prepositions, then; they matter.

PRACTICE OPPORTUNITIES

Is the underlined word a preposition or a verb particle? (Hint, if it's a particle, you'll be able to move it and the sentence will remain well formed.)

- *We have sent <u>out</u> all the letters.*
- *Several people brought <u>up</u> that topic.*
- *Shauna slid <u>off</u> her chair.*
- *The plane flew <u>over</u> the North Pole.*
- *Keith will leave <u>on</u> the 12th.*

13

Conjunctions at junctions

SOMETHING TO THINK ABOUT

Can you start a sentence with a **conjunction**? Why or why not? Do you do it anyway?

Question: Can you start a sentence with *And* or *Because*?
Answer: Not according to strict grammarians. However, there is a certain elasticity of formal usage in academic, business, and other professional settings. For example, a *New Yorker* magazine article I was reading had three instances of *And* at the start of sentences in the last two paragraphs. To be fair, those were the only occurrences in a full-length article, but there they were in print.

The basics of conjunctions

Conjunctions indeed appear at junctions. They join together phrases and clauses. Remember that a **phrase** is a group of words without a subject–verb pair (hence, it can't stand alone as its own sentence); a **clause**, in contrast, is a group of words with a subject–verb pair. However, this property alone doesn't qualify a clause automatically for sentence status; it depends. Let's look a little more closely.

Chapter 14 has more on clauses.

There are two basic types of conjunctions. The first type is called the **coordinating conjunction**, and the second type is called the **subordinating conjunction**. Note the prefixes on these labels – *co* and *sub* – for that will help you keep their functions straight.

Uses of conjunctions

Coordinating conjunctions

When you coordinate an outfit, you put matching items together. Similarly, coordinating conjunctions put together like elements of a sentence. There are seven conjunctions in this category, and they are usually remembered by the acronym BOYSFAN (some prefer FANBOYS). They are listed in Table 13.1, along with their corresponding meanings.

Table 13.1: Coordinating conjunctions and meanings (BOYSFAN words)

But = opposite
Or = alternative
Yet = opposite
So = cause/effect
For = because
And = addition, progression
Nor = negative of *or*

Coordinating conjunctions can join together smaller sentences. The two sentences

Lars rides a bike

and

Alana drives a car

can be linked by quite a few of the BOYSFAN words. Which one you use, of course, will depend on the intended meaning. Using any BOYSFAN word to connect two smaller sentences creates a **compound sentence**. A compound sentence is made up of two clauses that can stand alone but are joined by a coordinating conjunction. Each side of the conjunction is called an **independent clause**: it contains a subject–verb pair and can stand alone as a sentence. An independent clause is also called a **simple sentence**.

When the use of a coordinating conjunction creates a compound sentence, we have used the BOYSFAN word in a *sentential* way. The units the conjunction is conjoining could be sentences on their own. And, for those of you keeping track of commas, a comma goes right before (not after) the BOYSFAN word in the sentential use.

Chapter 16 has more on comma use.

Coordinating conjunctions can also connect smaller pieces of language. Take the sentence

Lars rides a bike but doesn't like to drive.

We see a BOYSFAN word, but look to either side of it. The left side is an independent clause, but the right side isn't: *doesn't like to drive* is missing a subject. The same is true with

Lars rides an old bike and a new motorcycle.

The *and* doesn't link two independent clauses but instead two noun phrases. The way the coordinating conjunctions are being used here is in a *phrasal* way, linking phrases rather than sentences.

Lars rides an old bike and a new motorcycle,

then, is not compound; it is a *simple sentence*, made up of one independent clause. And as for commas? A comma does not go before a BOYSFAN word in the phrasal use, so there is no comma after *bike* in the sentences above.

Can you start a sentence with a BOYSFAN word? Not technically, because they are conjoining words and need to be in the middle of something. But it is done all the time (as in this sentence). A BOYSFAN word at the start of a sentence, though, might be considered too informal for some professional writing.

Subordinating conjunctions

Since clauses with subject–verb pairs that can stand alone are called independent, it follows that clauses that cannot stand alone are called dependent.

A **dependent clause** contains a subject–verb pair, but it doesn't convey a full thought. Now, this criterion of a sentence might not be clear. If I asked why you went to the gym and you answered, "Because it's abs day," you did give me a good enough reason. Grammatically, though, the answer is not complete. The word *because* promises two parts: a cause and an effect. In writing, such an answer would be labeled a **sentence fragment**. Of course it happens in speech all the time, and it would be odd if we had to repeat all questions we were asked before giving the answer. Especially in writing, though, dependent clauses standing alone will be flagged as sentence fragments.

Chapter 16 has more on sentence fragments.

Notice that if you delete *because*, you <u>do</u> have a complete sentence.

It's abs day

is an independent clause. So leaving out words doesn't always create sentence fragments. Here, the inclusion of *because* creates anticipation of more information than is actually supplied. You can start a sentence with *because*, but you need to finish the thought.

Because it's abs day, I got to the gym early.
Because it's Saturday, I slept late.

If you have a fragment, it signals a certain level of informality in your writing that you may not desire. I make use of fragments, for effect, in this book. Ultimately, be mindful of your intent.

Because is one of our other types of conjunctions, a **subordinating conjunction**. The inclusion of a subordinating conjunction at the start of a clause makes the clause dependent (related to the *sub*-prefix).

How are subordinating conjunctions different from coordinating ones? A coordinating conjunction sits at the juncture between phrases or clauses; a subordinating conjunction fuses with the clause that follows. In

Claudia drinks coffee because she likes the taste,

because she likes the taste is the full dependent clause, including the conjunction. A BOYSFAN word is never part of a clause; it's the piece of tape holding the two clauses together.

Another difference between the two types of conjunctions is that sentences can start with subordinating conjunctions (e.g. *because*), but they are only half-complete until you add the independent clause.

Conjunctions at junctions

Let's look at some more *because* sentences.

Because she ran out of coffee, Tanya had no energy.

Here we have the following configuration:

Because she ran out of coffee = dependent clause,

made up of a subordinating conjunction at the start of the clause. Then we have a comma, and then

Tanya had no energy = the independent clause.

Remember you can't stop after the *because* clause without creating a sentence fragment. We can also flip the clauses around:

Tanya had no energy because she ran out of coffee.

We now have the configuration independent clause first, <u>no</u> comma, and then dependent clause (starting with subordinating conjunction). Which clause comes first is up to you, but if the dependent clause comes first, there is a comma after the full dependent clause (some books call for commas before contrast conjunctions); if the independent clause comes first, there is no comma needed. This type of sentence, made up of both an independent and dependent clause (regardless of order), is called a **complex sentence**.

There are too many subordinating conjunctions to form a memorable acronym, but Table 13.2 lists many of the commonly used ones, categorized by type of information being conveyed.

Table 13.2: Subordinating conjunctions

Causality (*because, so that, since*)
Possibility (*if, unless, whether*)
Time (*before, after, when, while*)
Contrast (*although, even though*)

We can also combine conjunction use so that a sentence is **compound-complex**, as in

> *Harry rode to school, but his tire blew because he went over a pothole.*

Can you explain why this sentence is both compound and complex?

Table T (see Cheat Sheet at the back of the book) reviews what types of sentences are formed when using these two types of conjunctions.

Some extra information

We called a clause formed by the use of a subordinating conjunction a dependent clause. Some books use the term "subordinating clause," instead. Whatever term you use (I like dependent clause), there are three types:

1 a clause starting with a subordinating conjunction, as we have been discussing;
2 a relative clause;
3 a complement clause.

> Chapter 14 has more on relative and complement clauses.

With all these conjunction choices, we are able to vary the length of our sentences, their structure, and the general rhythm of our speech and writing.

133

PRACTICE OPPORTUNITIES

Identify the conjunction type and the sentence type in the following sentences.

- *Monica plays the banjo but never in front of an audience.*
- *Suzy plays the drums, and her kit is in the basement.*
- *Katie plays the piano since her parents are very musical, and she is grateful for their support.*

14

Relative clauses (and more clauses and phrases)

SOMETHING TO THINK ABOUT

Do you have a history of using *which* and teachers telling you to use *that*? Or perhaps vice versa?

Question: Is it *I bought a book which won an award* or . . . *that won an award*?

Answer: *That.* Since we need to establish the exact book being discussed, what we need is a restrictive relative clause.

The basics of the relative clause

Like more than one aspect of English grammar, the *which/that* distinction is being blurred in daily use. I will give you the standard rule, but then you'll put down this book and find many instances in speech and print of that rule being contradicted. In fact, my guess is that the *which/that* distinction will not be alive in 50 years. For now, though, here's the story.

Which and *that* are two of a handful of words called **relative pronouns.** Table 14.1 gives the full list of relative pronouns.

Table 14.1: All relative pronouns

That
Which
Who
Whom
Whose

(Some books include *where* and *when* as relative pronouns, as in *We live in NYC, where you get the best pizza; I like the time of day when the streets are empty*. Other books, like this one, consider *where* and *when* subordinating conjunctions.)

> *Chapter 10 has more on pronouns.*
>
> *Chapter 13 has more on conjunctions and dependent clauses.*

Relative pronouns introduce a type of dependent clause embedded in a larger sentence frame. This type of dependent clause is called a **relative clause**. Remember that dependent clauses can't stand on their own as full sentences; neither can a relative clause. Here are some sentences containing relative clauses; note that a sentence can't *be* a relative clause, only *contain* one.

Jake won the prize, which the millionaire donated.

The part of the sentence that can't stand alone is *which the millionaire donated*. It's a clause because it has a subject–verb pair, but it doesn't have enough information on its own to allow it to be an independent clause.

What makes a relative clause and relative pronoun "relative"? Relative clauses give extra information related to something in the main clause of the sentence (sometimes called the "matrix sentence"). Further, the relative pronouns that introduce relative clauses don't have fixed meanings. In our sentence about Jake, the relative pronoun *which* refers to (has as its antecedent) the noun *prize* in the independent clause of the sentence (*which = the prize*). In another sentence, that same relative pronoun can refer to something else, as in

Jake ate a big meal, which he paid for with his prize money (which = a big meal).

Uses of the relative clause

Let's now take the sentence above with *which* and substitute *that* to see if anything changes:

Jake won the prize that the millionaire donated.

First of all, the comma disappeared. And believe it or not, the meaning of the sentence changed. When we used *which* as the relative pronoun, we were creating what is called a **non-restrictive relative clause** (NRC). We didn't need to restrict the pool of prizes we were discussing; there is only one prize, a comma follows, and now I will tell you a bit more about the prize (it was donated by a rich person).

By using the relative pronoun *that*, however, we have created a **restrictive relative clause** (RRC): we need to restrict the pool of prizes that we are talking about, i.e. tell more about the prize to narrow down which prize is being discussed. In other words, there were several prizes, but Jake won the particular one that the rich person donated.

Our NRC was preceded by a comma; the comma signals that the additional information in the relative clause is kind of parenthetical since we know which prize we are discussing, and we are then getting some additional information. In contrast, our RRC didn't call for the comma because the sentence hadn't conveyed which prize we wanted to discuss, and we needed that relative clause information to make ourselves clear. So we didn't separate the two clauses with a comma.

Does all this matter? Well, to make our ideas as clear as possible, yes. Take these two sentences:

Women who are smart study grammar. (RRC)
Women, who are smart, study grammar. (NRC)

The first sentence contains an RRC; that is, we are restricting the pool of women we are discussing: only those smart ones. In the second sentence, with an NRC, we already know whom we are talking about. In this case, all women – and, by the way, they are smart.

Note that in these sentences we make use of another relative pronoun, *who*, and it is the same in both sentences. There is no *which/that* contrast to worry about; however, the restrictive vs. non-restrictive nature of the relative clause can now only be signaled by the punctuation. The NRC is surrounded by commas since it is in the middle of the main sentence. Commas, again, are working like parentheses. If an NRC is at the end of the sentence, only one comma is needed to separate it from the main clause; if it is in the middle, then commas are needed on both sides of the relative clause.

> *Chapter 16 has more on commas.*

There are a few limits on the behavior of RRCs and NRCs. When the subject of a sentence is a proper noun or a pronoun, the sentence can't contain an RRC. So we can't have

*Molly interviewed Keith who was the class spokesman.

or

Molly interviewed him who was the class spokesman.

(Remember * means non-occurring.)

We can assume that there is only one *Keith* or *him* being discussed, so we don't need to narrow the pool of possible candidates.

The limit on use of an NRC involves indefinite pronouns. Here, we do want to limit who we are discussing:

Molly interviewed everyone, who witnessed the incident.

Since not everyone in the world was a witness, we need an RRC to clarify the meaning (so no comma).

Let's now look at how relative clauses are formed and at several more subcategories of relative clauses that exist. Relative clauses have as their original, base form two smaller independent clauses with a noun that occurs in both clauses. As an example, let's go back to Jake and the prize, and we'll use the non-restrictive version.

Jake won the prize, which the millionaire donated.

The two independent clause components (which I will call smaller sentences) are

Smaller sentence 1: *Jake won the prize.*
Smaller sentence 2: *The millionaire donated the prize.*

The noun that is present in both sentences is *the prize*. Here are the steps to creating a sentence with a relative clause.

• One occurrence of the duplicate noun gets changed to a relative pronoun.

- We line up the noun and the corresponding relative pronoun so that they are side by side, with the noun first and the relative pronoun following.
- The clause with the new relative pronoun becomes the relative clause and gets embedded in the other sentence, which becomes the main sentence frame.

We'll choose *the prize* in smaller sentence 2 to convert to a relative pronoun. Figure 14.1 illustrates all these moves.

- Conversion of noun to relative pronoun:
  Jake won the prize. The millionaire donated which.

- Line up noun and relative pronoun:
  Jake won the prize + which the millionaire donated.

- Embed clause with relative pronoun into first clause (with comma):
  Jake won the prize, which the millionaire donated.

Figure 14.1: Creation of a relative clause (object type)

We have formed a type of relative clause called an **object relative clause**. Object relative clauses give more information about the object of the main sentence. In the example above, the object being modified is the direct object. In the following sentence, the relative clause gives us more information about the indirect object of the main sentence:

Deanna taught French to the boy who won the prize.

Object relative clauses can be restrictive or non-restrictive. (Figure 14.1 shows the non-restrictive version.)

A different transformation could have happened with our two independent clauses, though. What if the overlapping word in smaller sentence 1 instead of 2 changed to the relative pronoun? Figure 14.2 illustrates this conversion.

- Conversion of noun to relative pronoun:
  Jake won which. The millionaire donated the prize.

- Line up noun and relative pronoun:
  The millionaire donated the prize + which Jake won.

- Embed clause with relative pronoun into first clause (with comma):
  The millionaire donated the prize, which Jake won.

Figure 14.2: Creation of another relative clause (object type)

In this conversion, the main clause and the relative clause are flipped from the earlier sentence about Jake (since the noun comes before the newly created relative pronoun). The relative pronoun is still giving us information about the direct object (*prize*), so it is also an object relative clause. And we have maintained the non-restrictive meaning of the relative clause (we already know which prize is being discussed).

Now take the sentence

The millionaire donated the prize that Jake won.

This is the RRC version of the sentence in Figure 14.2. It uses the relative pronoun *that* with no commas; the meaning is that there are several prizes, and we are narrowing our discussion to just one of them. The conversion would be the same as in Figure 14.2, but we would choose the relative pronoun *that* and use no commas.

Let's take two different smaller sentences now, where the overlapping noun is the subject of each sentence:

Smaller sentence 3: *The prize is worth $2000.*
Smaller sentence 4: *The prize is a trip to Hawaii.*

The overlapping noun is *the prize*. Can you convert these two smaller sentences into a sentence with a relative clause? Can you convert two different ways?

Figures 14.3 and 14.4 show us two ways to convert these smaller sentences into larger ones containing non-restrictive relative clauses. Figure 14.3 places the relative pronoun in smaller sentence 4. Figure 14.4 places the relative pronoun in smaller sentence 3.

The conversion steps in both Figures 14.3 and 14.4 have created NRCs: there is only one prize under discussion, and now we learn a little more about it. If we had to narrow down the list of possible prizes being discussed, we would use the relative pronoun *that* and no commas. All other conversion steps would be the same.

- Conversion of noun to relative pronoun:
  The prize is worth $2000 + which is a trip to Hawaii.

- Line up noun and relative pronoun:
  The prize + which is a trip to Hawaii + is worth $2000.

- Embed clause with relative pronoun into first clause (with commas): this step was taken care of when we lined up the noun and its corresponding relative pronoun.
  The prize, which is a trip to Hawaii, is worth $2000.

Figure 14.3: Creation of a relative clause (subject type)

- Conversion of noun to relative pronoun:
  Which is worth $2000. The prize is a trip to Hawaii.

- Line up noun and relative pronoun:
  The prize + which is worth $2000 + is a trip to Hawaii.

- Embed clause with relative pronoun into first clause (with commas): this step was taken care of when we lined up the noun and its corresponding relative pronoun.
  The prize, which is worth $2000, is a trip to Hawaii.

Figure 14.4 Creation of another relative clause (subject type)

Relative clauses (and more clauses and phrases)

The relative clauses in these last two conversions, though, don't modify the object of the main sentence; they modify the subject. Thus, these are **subject relative clauses**.

(Some linguists use the terms "object relative clause" and "subject relative clause" in a different way: to signal the role of the relative pronoun in the relative clause itself – as its object or subject – regardless of what the full clause modifies in the main sentence.)

What if the overlapping noun is the subject of one sentence and the object of another? We can convert the two smaller sentences into a sentence containing either an object or a subject relative clause. Let's go back to Jake, the prize, and the millionaire.

Smaller sentence 5: *Jake won the prize.*
Smaller sentence 6: *The prize was donated by the millionaire.*

(Yes, sentence 6 is in the passive voice.)

We can get two different larger sentences from smaller sentences 5 and 6. Try to write them out and identify them before you read the list below.

- *Jake won the prize, which was donated by the millionaire.* (object relative clause, non-restrictive)
- *Jake won the prize that was donated by the millionaire.* (object relative clause, restrictive)
- *The prize, which Jake won, was donated by the millionaire.* (subject relative clause, non-restrictive)
- *The prize that Jake won was donated by the millionaire.* (subject relative clause, restrictive)

So far we have seen relative pronouns *which*, *that*, and *who* in action. *Which* and *that* tend to be used when the antecedent is an inanimate object. *Who* and *whom* are used when the antecedent is a person; *who* = subject of sentence and *whom* = object of sentence.

In the blurring of *which* and *that*, I think *which* is winning. In other words, people are using *which* in both restrictive and non-restrictive relative clauses. Further, *who* and *that* are blurring:

The student that passed the exam left the room happy.

My inclination is to use *who* since it's a person being discussed. But *that* is in use as well.

Whose is a possessive, so we can say

The cat, whose tail is thick, sheds all over the furniture

or

The couch, whose cushions are black, shows all the cat hair.

Whose, then, is used for both animate and inanimate antecedents; in formal English, though, many would reword the couch example, above, to avoid linking *whose* to an inanimate object.

You want to make sure with relative clauses that the entity they are modifying is clear. Take this sentence:

Sally told me that Jim is a political science major, which pleases me.

The relative pronoun *which* is ambiguous in this construction: does it relate to Sally's telling of the fact about Jim or to the fact itself?

Reduced relative clause

In some situations, we have the option of reducing relative clauses by deleting the relative pronoun. This leads to what is called a

reduced relative clause. When can we delete the relative pronoun? Reduction is possible in a restrictive relative clause (but not non-restrictive) in which the relative pronoun is followed by the subject of the dependent clause.

We need some examples.

Full relative clause: *The picture that Billie painted was in the Cubist style.*

We can also say

Reduced relative clause: *The picture Billie painted was in the Cubist style.*

The full relative clause is *that Billie painted*. Relative pronoun *that* is followed by *Billie*, and she is the subject of the relative clause, so we can drop the *that*. (Notice that the relative clause being reduced is restrictive. If the sentence was *The picture, which Billie painted, was in the Cubist style*, we couldn't delete the relative pronoun.)

The picture that made the cover of Art News *was in the Cubist style*

can't be reduced to

*The picture made the cover of Art News *was in the Cubist style.*

Why not? Relative pronoun *that* is not followed by a subject. Instead, it <u>is</u> the subject of the relative clause.

Ready for an exception? If the relative pronoun is the subject of the relative clause it is in – either an RRC or NRC – <u>and</u> it is followed by the verb *to be*, you can delete both the relative pronoun and the verb. Take the sentence below:

Relative clauses (and more clauses and phrases)

Full relative clause: *The cat that is sitting in the window is bird watching.*

(Notice no commas, since we are restricting the pool of cats we are talking about.) Both *that* and *is* can be deleted to get

Reduced relative clause: *The cat sitting in the window is bird watching.*

Reducing a relative clauses can result in what is called an **appositive**.

Full relative clause: *James Levine, who is a famous conductor, is taking a sabbatical.*

This relative clause is non-restrictive; remember, with proper nouns there is no doubt whom we are discussing, and the NRC supplies modifying information. Further, we can reduce this relative clause because (1) *who* is the subject, and (2) it is followed by a form of *to be*:

Reduced relative clause: *James Levine, a famous conductor, is taking a sabbatical.*

That middle phrase (reduced from the relative clause) is our appositive, and it supplies further identifying information about the subject. That is what an appositive does.

Chapter 16 has more on appositives.

Reducing relative clauses is another way we can vary our sentence structures. However, reduction can also result in some difficulty for readers or listeners. I now give you the world's most famous "garden-path sentence," a type of sentence that leads us down a path to a dead end and makes us re-process the sentence:

The horse raced past the barn fell.

Does this sentence make sense to you? It does if we think of its full relative clause:

The horse that was raced past the barn fell.

A relative clause is reduced by deleting the subject relative pronoun *that*, as well as the following form of *to be*.

Of course we don't want to create ambiguous sentences, so check for clarity when you delete relative pronouns.

Tables U and V, in the Cheat Sheet at the back of the book, summarize all the relative clause types we have been discussing.

Look-alikes: not relative pronouns

Complement clause

We've already seen a few other types of *that* besides the relative pronoun. In

That's a great idea,

that is a dummy subject. The word *that* can also act as a demonstrative pronoun, as in

That (pointing to the prize) *was donated by the millionaire.*

Relative clauses (and more clauses and phrases)

Chapter 4 has more on dummy subjects.

Chapter 10 has more on pronouns.

That can also be what's called a **complementizer**, introducing another type of dependent clause called a **complement clause**, a mini-sentence inside a larger sentence frame. For example:

I know that you love grammar.

In this sentence, *that* does not introduce a relative clause. Why? Because it doesn't act as a relative pronoun; we can't assign a noun in the main sentence as its antecedent. Instead, it's signaling that another clause is about to appear. The complementizer *that* introduces the clause *you love grammar*. The clause (with complementizer) is dependent: it can't stand alone. (Complement clauses are actually noun clauses. More on that below. In addition, there are a handful of other words besides *that* in the complementizer category, but I won't go into them.)

Students over the years have carried over to my classroom the preferences of their various high school teachers: some say delete the *that*; others say insert the *that*. What is this *that*? It's the complementizer, and it introduces the clause to follow. But sometimes, it can be deleted.

I know that you love grammar → *I know you love grammar.*

As with reduced relative clauses, be sure to check for clarity before reducing complement clauses. Some reading specialists say we process sentences better when the complementizer is present. So in the sentence

I know you love grammar,

we might mistakenly process the first three words as an S–V–O string, mistaking the word *you* for the direct object: *I know you*. We then get to *love grammar* and have to re-process the sentence.

All types of clauses

At this point, let's summarize all types of clauses we've discussed so far, and add a few new ones.

Clause types covered already

Independent clause
Dependent clause starting with subordinating conjunction
Restrictive relative clause
Non-restrictive relative clause
Reduced relative clause
Complement clause

Clause types about to be covered

Adjectival clause (and phrase)
Adverbial clause (and phrase)
Noun clause

Adjectives and adverbs as phrases and clauses

Adjectives and adverbs can still do their work as modifiers when they are part of a larger unit, either in a phrase or a clause. A phrase is a group of words without a subject–verb pair; a clause is a group of words with a subject–verb pair that might be a full sentence (independent clause) or not (dependent clause).

> Chapters 12 and 13 have more on phrases and clauses.

Adjectival phrase

The teacher <u>from the local college</u> shops at the food co-op.

Here, a prepositional phrase is modifying the noun *teacher* and thus acting as an adjective.

Adjectival clause

The teacher <u>who just moved to Ohio</u> misses the coast.

(A clause, in this case also a relative clause, modifies the noun *teacher*.)

Adverbial phrase

Adverbs modify verbs. A whole adverbial phrase can also modify a verb:

Fiona opened the package <u>with extreme care</u>.

Here the prepositional phrase *with extreme care* is also acting as an adverbial phrase, describing the manner in which Fiona did the opening.

> *We stood <u>in line for an hour</u>* (or in New Yorkese: *We stood <u>on</u> line for an hour*).

Here, the prepositional phrases *in/on line* and *for an hour* convey place and time information, modifying the action of *stood*.

Adverbial clause

An adverb in a clause, acting as an adverbial clause, can be seen in the sentence

> *Fiona opened the package <u>after she checked who sent it</u>.*

After she checked who sent it is a dependent clause (it starts with a subordinating conjunction), and it modifies the action of opening the package.

The basics of the noun clause

You can guess from the name that a noun clause is a group of words containing a subject–verb pair that functions as a noun in a sentence. Since a noun can function as a subject, object, or complement in the predicate, a noun clause can also fill the subject, object, and complement slots in a sentence.

Chapter 6 has more on complements in predicates.

Uses of the noun clause

Noun clause as subject

That Brendan scored the highest on the exam didn't surprise anyone.

The full entity *That Brendan scored the highest on the exam* is the noun clause, not any one particular word. Here and in the next example, these noun clauses are also complement clauses, starting with complementizer *that*.

Noun clause as direct object

I heard *that Brendan scored the highest on the exam*.

Again, a full noun clause is what is being heard, i.e. is the direct object.

Noun clause as complement

In Chapter 6, I gave the sentence

Allen is a mathematician

as an example of a subject complement (remember we could rewrite as *Allen = a mathematician*). The subject complement was the noun phrase *a mathematician*, not a full clause. We can also have

Allen's hope is that mathematics will become more popular in the coming years.

Now we have a full noun clause as a subject complement.

This chapter discusses a lot of terms that start with "comp," so it might be helpful to list all of them:

Complementizer: the word *that*, introducing a dependent clause called a complement clause.

Complement clause: a type of dependent clause starting with a complementizer such as *that*.

Complement of the predicate: gives more information, in the form of an adjective or noun, about the subject or direct object of the sentence.

One more type of clause: take the sentence

I wonder what time it is.

Here, we are not really asking a question, so the structure of the sentence stays in declarative subject–verb order (and notice no question mark). The clause *what time it is* is called a **pseudo question**. Some forms of English allow for the interrogative word order that inverts subject and verb: *I wonder what time is it* (sometimes written with a question mark following). Such a construction, however, is not standard.

PRACTICE OPPORTUNITIES

Evaluate the use of relative pronouns in the following sentences. Convert any non-standard to standard forms.

- *Carissa decided to take the class which meets on Mondays.*
- *Brian chats with friends that have Facebook accounts.*
- *Loren knows that the secret is in the box.*
- *Brooklyn, that is the most crowded borough, is home to Prospect Park.*
- *The recording sounded best was a vinyl album.*

15

Misaligned modifiers

SOMETHING TO THINK ABOUT

Do you think there is anything odd about the following sentence: "Sitting in the classroom, the clock ticked loudly"?

Question: What is a dangling or misplaced modifier, and why is it to be avoided?

Answer: Modifiers modify something. If their placement doesn't line up with the part of the sentence to which they relate, the modifiers are dangling or misplaced.

The basics of misaligned modifiers

Some grammar books differentiate between a *dangling* modifier (one that has no anchor at all in the sentence to modify) and a *misplaced* modifier (the modifying word is in the wrong part of the sentence). I will merge these two terms and call them both **misaligned modifiers**. Further, several units of language can act as modifiers: present and past participle phrases; prepositional phrases; and infinitive verb phrases.

Misaligned present participle phrase

What is going on in the sentence about the clock, above? We can say that something at the start of the sentence is not properly anchored to the rest of the sentence.

Sitting in the classroom is a **present participle phrase**. Remember a phrase is a group of words without a subject–verb pair; and that the present participle is formed from the base of the verb and an *–ing* ending. The present participle is *sitting* and the phrase is *sitting* and everything that goes with it.

The present participle phrase is at the beginning of the sentence, but what is its connection to the second part of the sentence? In other words, who or what was sitting? The word right after the comma – the word that starts the independent clause – should be the anchor to that beginning phrase. Right now, we have the clock doing the sitting. While we probably have no trouble understanding that the student (or teacher), not the clock, is sitting and listening to the clock tick, a different meaning has been created by not appropriately aligning the two parts of the sentence.

Misaligned: *Sitting in the classroom, the clock ticked loudly.*
Better: *Sitting in the classroom, we heard the clock ticking loudly.*

Misaligned past participle phrase

The example above shows a misaligned present participle phrase. Another phrase that can be misaligned – that is, attached in a confusing way to the main sentence – is a **past participle phrase**.

Remember that the past participle is the third form of a verb when you think of its triplets (*see, saw, seen*).

Misaligned: *Seen on TV, we went out and bought the exercise machine.*

We, however, weren't what was on TV.

Better: *Seen on TV, the exercise machine tempted us to buy it.*

Or, if we don't want a passive sentence,

Better: *We bought the exercise machine after we saw it on TV.*

Here is another example:

Misaligned: *Frozen for weeks, we finally defrosted the turkey.*

Clearly, we weren't frozen for weeks; the turkey was. Yet, the word right after the comma is *we*, not the entity formerly frozen and being thawed.

Better: *Frozen for weeks, the turkey was finally defrosted (or finally thawed).*

Misaligned prepositional phrase

Prepositional phrases consist of a preposition and its object, either a noun or a pronoun. We have to be careful with the placement of prepositional phrases, too.

Misaligned: *With a loud ring, Colin woke to the alarm.*

Given this wording, Colin was the one ringing loudly.

> **Better**: *With a loud ring, the alarm woke Colin,*

or

> **Better**: *Colin was woken by the loud ring of the alarm,*

or

> **Better**: *Colin woke to the loud ring of the alarm.*

Misaligned infinitive verb phrase

> **Misaligned**: *To fit properly, you should try on shoes in the evening.*

The word at the start of the independent clause (right after the comma) should be the anchor for the infinitive verb phrase.

> **Better**: *To fit properly, shoes should be tried on in the evening*

or, if you don't like the passive voice,

> **Better**: *Try shoes on in the evening for a better fit.*

We can also put *shoes* in the infinitive phrase:

> **Better**: *For shoes to fit properly, you should try them on in the evening.*

The message, then, about modifying phrases: make sure they align. Modifiers can easily be realigned without much surgery to the sentence or loss of meaning.

As a teacher of writing, I see lots of misaligned modifiers. Writers often get a bit distracted when they don't start a sentence with the main subject. While the ambiguities of such sentences can be funny –

Eating raw fish out of a pail, we saw the polar bear in the Central Park Zoo

– and easily cleared up by logic, sometimes the wrong meaning can be conveyed:

Hot in the summer sun, the team drank the Gatorade.

Either entity (team or drink) could be hot here.

PRACTICE OPPORTUNITIES

Identify what type of phrase might be misplaced in the following sentences and correct the wording of the sentence.

- *Floating in the soup, Treb found a bug.*
- *Floating in the pool, Treb felt relaxed.*
- *Written ages ago, the author dusted off the manuscript.*

16

Commas: more than pauses

SOMETHING TO THINK ABOUT

Where do you put commas when you are writing? Do you use them "correctly"?

Question: How long does a sentence need to be to become a **run-on**?
Answer: The number of words has little to do with whether or not a sentence is a run-on. If two independent clauses are not separated by the correct punctuation, you have a run-on sentence.

The basics of the comma

We already know something about commas. Chapter 14 discussed commas as they are used with relative clauses. I also brought up commas in Chapter 13 when we looked at coordinating and subordinating conjunctions.

So you are getting the idea that there are rules for comma use. Writers sometimes think a comma goes where a speaker would pause. That is not a good rule of thumb. Don't worry, however: you can be a fine writer and bad with commas. (My first-year English teacher in college gave me a B+ instead of an A on a paper because, she wrote in the margin, "*Your comma use is horrible.*" So to some, it matters – to me anyway; my husband is still shaking his head at my reaction to a B+.)

Uses of the comma

Here to prevent you from getting such marginalia in the future are the rules for comma use, in no particular order, but all together in one chapter. (To be honest, I have left out a few uses, such as commas with i.e. and e.g. since style books differ in this regard.) As you'll see, several of these rules rely on concepts we discussed earlier.

Rule 1: Use a comma right before a coordinating conjunction (BOYSFAN word) when the conjunction links two independent clauses in a compound sentence; in other words, when it is being used sententially. If it's being used phrasally, don't use a comma.

Use a comma: *Sherise joined the committee, but she is not sure if she wants to be the chairperson.*

Don't use a comma: *Sherise joined the committee but is not sure she wants to be the chairperson.*

Rule 2: Use a comma after a dependent clause when an independent clause follows in a complex sentence. If the independent clause comes first, don't use a comma.

Use a comma: *Since the committee meets every night, Sherise is not sure she wants to be chairperson.*

Don't use a comma: *Sherise is not sure she wants to be chairperson since the committee meets every night.*

Rule 3: Use commas to set apart a non-restrictive relative clause from the main sentence. If the clause is in the middle of the sentence, you need commas on both sides of the relative clause; if it's at the end of the sentence, you only need one comma. Do not use commas to separate a restrictive relative clause from the main sentence.

Use a comma: *Chloe keeps her pet snails in her room, which is at least far from the kitchen.*

Her favorite snail, which is the one she got for her last birthday, gets special treatment.

Don't use a comma: *Chloe's favorite snail is the one that she got for her last birthday.*

Rule 4: Use commas when listing.

Eri needs to go shopping for paper, pens, and a new backpack.

That final comma is not always used. It is called the **serial comma**. (Some books call it the Harvard or the Oxford comma.) Different style guides and teachers have different preferences about the serial comma. Check style books or in-house guides, or with your professor about its use.

I happen to like the option. Note the difference between

The guest list includes Judi, Teresa and Lou vs. *Judi, Teresa, and Lou.*

The former gives a greater sense (to me) of *Teresa and Lou* being a couple, or at least a unit, compared to when the serial comma is present.

Rule 5: Use a comma after introductory material in a sentence that delays the subject.

In the morning, Doris jogs up the hill.

Jogging up the hill, Doris decided to get new sneakers.

Chapter 15 has more on modifying phrases and clauses introducing a sentence.

Commas: more than pauses

Rule 6: Use commas to set off parenthetical information (unless you are using parentheses or another form of punctuation).

The morning, by the way, is the best time for Doris to go jogging.

Rule 7: Use commas to set off an appositive. An **appositive** is extra identifying information about an entity already mentioned in the sentence. For example:

Kevin, our college's web master, works on the 4th floor.

The inserted material *our college's web master* is an appositive, extra information about Kevin. (Keen readers will also note that the appositive here is a reduced relative clause.)

Rule 8: Use commas to set off direct address material.

I'll tell you, Kate, the pizza at Grimaldi's is worth the wait.

(I am speaking directly to Kate.)

Rule 9: Use commas in dates. Use commas after the day and then after the whole piece of information.

Oct. 9, 1940, was the day John Lennon was born.

Rule 10: Use commas in addresses and after the whole address.

John and Yoko moved to 1 West 72 Street, New York, in the 1970s.

Rule 11: Use commas with a series of adjectives.

The long, boring, low-budget movie finally ended.

Note here that you don't use a comma after the last adjective.

Rule 12: Use a comma before quoted material.

Mel said, "I am a vegan."

Run-on sentences, comma splices, fused sentences, and sentence fragments

To return to our question at the start of the chapter, how long is a run-on sentence? Some writers try to "fix" run-on sentences by ending them too soon, thus creating another structure considered an error in formal writing: a **sentence fragment**. **Run-on sentences** really aren't about the number of words; they are created when two independent clauses aren't separated by the right punctuation mark. Note that you can't have a run-on in speech. It's considered a writing error, more specifically a mechanics error in that we aren't technically even in the realm of grammar when we discuss punctuation.

Some grammar texts say there are two types of run-on sentences: (1) a **comma splice**, created by using a comma, too weak a punctuation mark, between independent clauses; and (2) a **fused sentence**, where there is no punctuation at all at the junction. To me, *run-on* and *fused* refer to the same thing, and *comma splice* is a special type of run-on. No matter the label, the right punctuation mark is needed when you are joining clauses together.

Take this sentence:

Jenna knits, she's talented.

This is a four-word sentence, but it's a comma splice type of run-on because each half is an independent clause (has a subject–verb pair and can stand on its own), and the comma is too weak a punctuation mark to be at the junction. The writer has several fix-up choices:

Jenna knits. She is talented.

Here a period separates the two clauses.

Jenna knits, and she is talented.

Here we use a coordinating conjunction in its sentential function. Note that the comma remains.

Jenna knits; she is talented.

Ah, the **semi-colon**. We saw semi-colons in Chapter 11 being used with conjunctive adverbs. I like to tell students that the semi-colon is perfectly designed: half comma, half period. The period part means that you are separating two independent clauses; the comma part signals that the two clauses convey related ideas. (There are a few other ways semi-colons are used, especially in lists where commas appear within items, but we won't go further into that punctuation here.)

Let's look at a longer sentence:

Jenna knits all her own sweaters whenever she needs to save some money.

A writer suspecting that this sentence is "too long" might put a period after *sweaters* and thus create a sentence fragment from the second half of the sentence.

Whenever she needs to save some money.

Commas: more than pauses

The sentence fragment has a subject–verb pair, but it also begins with a subordinating conjunction. In other words, it's a dependent clause. It needs to be attached to the independent clause. The original sentence, 13 words long with no comma, was correctly punctuated.

You can find plenty of fragments in print. In a *New York Times* article about Chicago hotels, I found this sentence: "On State Street, at the northern end of the loop." In fact, there are numerous examples of fragments in this very book. For example, just a few paragraphs ago, you read, "Ah, the semi-colon." I was trying to strike an informal, conversational tone by keeping that fragment as its own sentence.

> *Chapter 13 has more on sentence fragments.*

Here's another example of a writer trying to "fix" what he or she suspects is a run-on by inserting a comma:

The students took their last exam on Thursday afternoon, they now have the whole summer to relax.

Can you see what is awry here? We have a **comma splice,** i.e. two independent clauses separated by a mere comma. Try to fix this comma splice in the several different ways discussed above.

PRACTICE OPPORTUNITIES

The following sentences have incorrect punctuation. Correct any errors and explain what was wrong.

- *Charlie plays pool every Thursday. Something he enjoys.*
- *Sharon also likes to play pool, however, she never has the free time to get to the pool hall.*
- *They should form a team. The reason being that they are so talented.*

17

Apostrophes:
dueling functions

A sign in a deli says, "Buy 12 bagel's and get 2 free." What's going on here?

Question: Is it _it's_ or _its?_
Answer: It depends. _It's_ is the contraction of _it + has_ or _it + is_; _its_ is the possessive form.

The basics of the apostrophe

The apostrophe causes confusion because it has three functions: ownership as with a possessive, **contraction** when letters are deleted, and – less often – pluralization. Let's take these functions one at a time.

Uses of the apostrophe

Possessive

We tend to think "apostrophe *s*" when we think of the possessive ending on a noun. What gets confusing is when the noun with the possessive marker already ends in an *s*, either because it is a plural or just spelled that way, like the noun *boss*. Does the "apostrophe *s*" go before or after an already existing *s* on a noun? Here's a trick: place the apostrophe where you think it should go, cover the apostrophe, and look to the left. The word will either be singular or plural. Do you see the form of the word you want?

Here's an example. My high school yearbook had a page devoted to

The <u>Girl's</u> Basketball Team.

If you cover the apostrophe and look to the left, you have the singular *girl*. That would be a one-girl team, not what the yearbook editors intended. They should have written

The <u>Girls'</u> Basketball Team.

Here's an exception: when I taught English at a fashion college, I got nowhere insisting that Men's Wear was two words when just a few blocks uptown, Macy's had a Menswear Department. I was able, however, to point out the apostrophe in the store's name: R. H. Macy's is shorthand for R. H. Macy's Department Store. (In many of the store's ads, the apostrophe is a star, but it's in the right place.)

In the yearbook example above, why is the possessive *girls'* and not *girls's*? Some people do write *girls's* (here's another bit of English in flux). However, some style guides give this general rule: for plural nouns ending in *s*, no double-*s* apostrophe (*girls'*, not *girls's*); but for singular nouns ending in *s*, some guides leave it up to the writer. So we can have *Thomas' car* or *Thomas's car*. Other guides prefer *Thomas's*. I've also seen rules that are less dependent on singular/plural and more on how the possessive noun sounds. Say it out loud. If the possessive form adds an extra syllable, then use an apostrophe + *s*. So:

No added syllable to the noun

I have two hours' worth of homework.

Here the possessive on *hours* doesn't add a syllable, so the addition of only an apostrophe is okay.

Added syllable to the noun

The book by Helen Fielding (and its movie title) uses this possessive rule:

Bridget Jones's Diary.

Take the sentence

The boss's memo arrived yesterday.

Here *boss* (the singular form) ends in *s*. When you make it possessive, you add a syllable. Thus, apostrophe and another *s* are used. To me, *boss's* has too many *s*'s (note the apostrophe I just used for the plural *s*'s; we'll come back to that). What if you were talking about more than one boss owning something? It's *bosses'* since the extra syllable is already there (and it's a plural-*s* noun to boot). Where there is choice about an extra *s*, it's best to be consistent and check your audience's preference.

By the way, if two people own something, as in

Tony and Sue's dog is named Boxy,

only the second noun gets the overt possessive marker. If each owns a dog with the same name, however, we have

Tony's and Sue's dogs are both named Boxy.

In Chapter 10, we went over pronouns that show possession; these possessive pronouns do not get an apostrophe:

The book is hers; the house is ours; the car is theirs.

We might be tempted to add that apostrophe because the possessive noun uses it (*Sarah's* matches up with *hers*), but the apostrophe isn't used in the pronoun set.

Contraction

When it comes to using an apostrophe to signal possessive vs. contraction in similar-looking words, contraction wins the apostrophe. What I mean by that is evident in the *it's* vs. *its* comparison, which began the chapter. The apostrophe in the word *it's* signals contraction, not possession. Why? Because contraction wins! (Even with the contracted *it's*, there is a choice: the contraction can mean *it is* or *it has*). If contraction wins, then the form without the apostrophe is the possessive meaning. So

It's = contraction, as in *It's hot out* and *It's been a long day.*

Its = possession, as in *The dog wagged its tail.*

Another pair similar to *it's* vs. *its* is *who's* vs. *whose*. Which meaning gets the apostrophe? The contraction wins!

Who's = *who* + *is* (*Who's there?*) or *who* + *has* (*Who's been there lately?*)

Whose = possessive (*Whose umbrella is this?*)

169

The same rule applies in all the possessive pronouns. There is no apostrophe in *theirs*, as I mentioned above. But the sound-alike pair *they're* and *their*? When it comes to a fight over the apostrophe, the contraction wins, so the form that gets the apostrophe is *they're*.

> *They're* = contraction of *they + are*.
>
> *Their* = *possessive*.

Of course there is a third form of *there*, meaning location. Think of this triple threat this way: *There* has *here* in it, so it refers to location. *They're* follows the contraction-wins rule, so it is *they + are*. *Their* has the word *heir* in it, as in heir to the throne, meaning ownership, so this *their* is the possessive meaning.

Pluralization

This chapter is full of rules of thumb. Another good rule of thumb is to assume a plural form does not get an apostrophe. Using apostrophes to mark plurality unnecessarily is a very common over-use of the mark, so you get signs like this at the bakery:

> *Buy 12 bagel's and get 2 free.*

The apostrophe is used in plurals, though, where the omission of the mark would make the sentence hard to read. For example,

> *There are two t's in her last name.*

I could write *two ts*, but it looks odd, and the meaning isn't entirely clear: does the name include two instances of *t* or two instances of *ts*? One style book I checked says to use a capital letter and no apostrophe in this situation (*Ts*).

Apostrophes: dueling functions

Another place you'll find apostrophe-plural is in abbreviations. Guidebooks disagree; one book I checked suggested

There are too many Ph.D.'s on the market right now.

Others, however, say don't use the apostrophe:

Too many Ph.D.s is the least of our problems.

Earlier I wrote that

John Lennon moved to New York City in the 1970s.

We could say he was in the city in the '70s. The apostrophe is to show that some numerals are missing (1970s). Some writers like to put an apostrophe after the year (the 1970's or '70's); the second apostrophe is not necessary. It's important that your own usage be consistent within a document. I should heed my own advice since I vacillate when it comes to pluralizing letters and numbers; for example, I would write

There are two o's in the name Oona,

where the apostrophe makes sense since "os" or even "Os" looks funny to me; and also

I find that 7's are lucky for me,

where it is not necessary since "7s" is not difficult to read. In Chapter 12, I wrote "up's" in the discussion of preposition and verb particles. *The New York Times* style book calls for no plural apostrophes in the phrase "dos and don'ts"; my fingers are itching to type "do's."

Apostrophes: dueling functions

The plural apostrophe is growing in usage. Take note of how often you see (or use) an apostrophe in a plural. I'll end with a sign I saw over a sink in a local restaurant:

Employees' must wash hand's after using restroom.

Can you map out the apostrophe use here?

PRACTICE OPPORTUNITIES

Fix the incorrect use of apostrophes in the sentences below.

* *The name of a Lucille Ball movie from the 1960's is "You'rs, Mine and Our's."*
* *Womens' shoes are on the fourth floor.*
* *The Number 6 Bus' wheels have fallen off.*

Who's vs. *Whose*? Fill in the blanks.

* ____ *book is this?*
* ____ *at the door?*

18

Applying the knowledge

Let's put all our knowledge together. Look at the paragraph below. Try to identify all non-standard forms and change to standard. The answers follow. Good luck!

On The Beatle's <u>The</u> <u>White</u> <u>Album</u>, they played together during a turbulent time. Having temporarily quit the band, Paul actually played drums instead of Ringo on "Dear Prudence." George Martin had to approve all the back-up musicians which recorded on the album. Including Eric Clapton. Thus, there were less people. Appearances got made by two girlfriends at the studio. Yoko Ono was the oldest, Linda McCartney was eight years younger. Linda took photographs from the control booth. Which was her job, however, the roll of snapshots weren't sufficient to capture the mixed emotions of the band. Neither of the famous lead singers who came from Liverpool were speaking to one another. None of the fans outside the studio were willing to believe that the band was having there problems. There's too many rumors for any to be credible, this was probably for the best, although The Beatles break-up had essentially begun. If we fans was to hear of a Paul and Ringo reunion, we'd line up for day's to buy tickets. It's legend lays in their combination of music and lyrics, we'll always love The Beatles.

Edited paragraph with comments

On The Beatles' <u>The</u> <u>White</u> <u>Album</u>, the four musicians played together during a turbulent time.

1 Apostrophe after full name *Beatles*.
2 *They* replaced with *the four musicians* since no antecedent for *they*.

Having temporarily quit the band, Ringo was replaced by Paul on drums for the song "Dear Prudence."

1 Dangling modifier. *Ringo* needs to go after comma.

George Martin had to approve all the back-up musicians who recorded on the album, including Eric Clapton.

1 Antecedent is *musicians*, so relative pronoun should be *who*.
2 No comma with a restrictive relative clause.
3 Need comma after *album* to fix sentence fragment.

Thus, there were fewer people in the studio than was usual.

1 The word *people* is a count noun so takes the quantifier *fewer*.
2 The word *fewer* is comparative, so we need to have something else to compare – than the usual number of people in the studio during a recording.

Two girlfriends made appearances at the studio.

1 Original wording is the informal *got* – passive.
2 The sentence works better with the agents in the subject slot, i.e. in the active voice.

Yoko Ono was older than Linda McCartney by eight years.

1　If discussing two people/objects/actions, use comparative: *older*, not *oldest*.
2　Fixed comma splice.

Linda was in the control booth taking photographs, which was her job.

1　The phrase *from the control booth* contains an ambiguous preposition: do we mean she photographed from there or moved photos away from that location? It's been reworded.
2　We need to fix the sentence fragment with a comma, not period, after *booth*. That comma also signals that the relative clause *which was her job* is non-restrictive.

However, the roll of snapshots wasn't sufficient to capture the mixed emotions of the band.

1　We need a new sentence starting with conjunctive adverb "however" to fix the comma splice. We need more than a comma; we could also use a semi-colon.
2　Subject–verb agreement needs to be fixed: *roll = wasn't.*

Neither of the famous lead singers . . . was speaking to each other.

1　Subject–verb agreement needs to be fixed: *neither = was.*
2　We use *one another* if talking about more than two people, and we use *each other* if talking about just two lead singers (assuming that John and Paul are the lead singers).

. . . famous lead singers, who came from Liverpool, was speaking to each other.

1   The relative clause needs to be non-restrictive since the fact that the singers came from Liverpool is not narrowing down the pool of possible musicians under discussion; it is just modifying information.

2   Note the commas around the non-restrictive relative clause.

None of the fans outside the studio was willing to believe that the band was having its problems.

1   Subject–verb agreement needs to be fixed: *none = was.*

2   The word *there* is not the possessive form.

3   And since *band* is singular, possessive *its* is needed instead (no apostrophe).

There were too many rumors for any to be credible.

1   The word *there's* needs to be *there + were*: plural since the grammatical subject is *rumors*; past tense to be consistent with the rest of the paragraph.

Ignoring the rumors was probably for the best although The Beatles' break-up had essentially begun.

1   The pronoun *this* is vague, so we need to add the clearer antecedent *ignoring the rumors.*

2   We have a comma splice because of the comma after *for any to be credible*; better to use a period.

3   We don't need a comma before subordinating conjunction *although*; some books say keep in comma.

4   We need an apostrophe after the full name of the group to show ownership: *The Beatles' break-up.*

If we fans were to hear of a Paul and Ringo reunion . . .

1 We want the subjunctive mood since this is a wished-for event.

    . . . we'd line up for days to buy tickets.

1 There should be no apostrophe for plural *days*.

    The musicians' legend lies in their combination of music and lyrics.

1 *Its* is being used in the possessive sense, so there should be no apostrophe.
2 However, since we have plural *their*, it's better to have a plural antecedent: *The musicians' legend . . .* Or we could go with the singular throughout: *the band's* and *its combination.*
3 We want the intransitive verb *lies*, not *lays*, since there is no direct object.

    We'll always love The Beatles.

1 We should make this a new sentence to fix a comma splice.
2 After compound and complex sentences, I like the punch of the final short simple sentence.

Corrected paragraph

On The Beatles' The White Album, the four musicians played together during a turbulent time. Having temporarily quit the band, Ringo was replaced by Paul on drums for the song "Dear Prudence." George Martin had to approve all the back-up musicians who recorded on the album, including Eric Clapton.

Thus, there were fewer people in the studio than was usual. Two girlfriends made appearances at the studio. Yoko Ono was older than Linda McCartney by eight years. Linda was in the control booth taking photographs, which was her job. However, the roll of snapshots wasn't sufficient to capture the mixed emotions of the band. Neither of the famous lead singers, who came from Liverpool, was speaking to each other. None of the fans outside the studio was willing to believe that the band was having its problems. There were too many rumors for any to be credible. Ignoring the rumors was probably for the best although The Beatles' break-up had essentially begun. If we fans were to hear of a Paul and Ringo reunion, we'd line up for days to buy tickets. The musicians' legend lies in their combination of music and lyrics. We'll always love The Beatles.

Further reading

Books about grammar that are worth reading

Good overall reference books

- Diana Hacker. 2010. *A Writer's Reference*. New York: Bedford/St. Martin's.
- Wynford Hicks. 2009. *The Basics of English Usage*. London: Routledge.
- Howard Jackson. 2002. *Grammar and Vocabulary: A resource book for students*. London: Routledge

NB: these books go beyond grammar and also discuss usage and mechanics.

Old timers

- R. W. Burchfield. 2004. *Fowler's Modern English Usage, Revised 3rd edition* (first edition by H. W. Fowler. Oxford University Press.)
- W. Strunk and E. B. White. 2000. *The Elements of Style, 4th edition*. Boston: Allyn and Bacon. (The 2008 edition celebrates the fiftieth anniversary of the book. There is also a 2005 edition with illustrations by Maira Kalman. And did you know this is the E. B. White who wrote *Charlotte's Web*?)

Note how many editions of these classics have appeared over the years, reinforcing the idea that what is "standard" changes with time.

Grammar texts for teachers and teachers-in-training

- Brock Haussamen (with Amy Benjamin, Martha Kolln, Rebecca S. Wheeler, and members of NCTE's Assembly for the Teaching of English Grammar). 2003. *Grammar Alive! A guide for teachers.* Urbana, IL: NCTE.
- Rei R. Noguchi. 1991. *Grammar and the Teaching of Writing: Limits and possibilities.* Urbana, IL: NCTE.
- Edgar H. Schuster. *Breaking the Rules: Liberating writers through innovative grammar instruction.* 2003. Portsmouth, NH: Heinemann.

Sentence diagramming

- Kitty Burns Florey. 2006. *Sister Bernadette's Barking Dog: The quirky history and lost art of diagramming sentences.* Orlando, FL: Harvest Books.

I thought about having a chapter in this text on diagramming, but then I decided that with diagramming, it's all or nothing; a single chapter wouldn't do. There are websites that will diagram any sentence you input. Burns Florey's book is partly how-to and partly history of the art of diagramming.

Burns Florey discusses the Reed and Kellogg approach. In modern syntactic theory, there are alternative ways to represent sentence structures visually. They can be found in:

- Jong-Bok Kim and Peter Sells. 2008. *English Syntax: An introduction.* Stanford, CA: CSL Publications.
- Andrew Radford. 2009. *An Introduction to English Sentence Structure.* Cambridge: Cambridge University Press.

- James D. Williams. 2005. *The Teacher's Grammar Book, 2nd edition*. Mahwah, NJ: Lawrence Erlbaum Associates.

Websites

These websites offer language views that are both prescriptive, in that Standard English is unquestioned as the only correct form of grammar; and more descriptive, in line with the field of linguistics. They all make for good reading.

- After Deadline http://topics.blogs.nytimes.com/tag/after-deadline (blog on the website of the *New York Times* about grammatical gray areas).
- Grammar Girl http://grammar.quickanddirtytips.com (grammar, writing, usage, mechanics).
- http://linguistlist.org (gigantic chat room for linguistics).
- http://www.chompchomp.com/exercises.htm (grammar exercises).
- http://www.ncsu.edu/linguistics/ncllp/index.php (North Carolina Project of Walt Wolfram; non-standard dialect documented in detail).
- William Safire. *On Language*. Safire, who died in 2009, wrote the "On Language" column in the *Sunday Magazine* of the *New York Times* for 30 years. The column continues with new contributors. The *New York Times* website offers back columns, starting from 1981: http://www.nytimes.com.
- *Vocabula Review* (http://vocabula.com). Their motto is "A society is generally as lax as its language," telling you these folks are fond of Standard English.

Answers to practice opportunity questions

Chapter 1

Divide the following sentences into subject and predicate.

Have you ever been to Hackensack?
(Subject = *you*; predicate = *have ever been to Hackensack*)

Who's there?
(Subject = *who*; predicate = *is there*)

Luz studied law and went to work for the city.
(Subject = *Luz*; predicate = *studied law and went to work for the city*)

Ashwin, a student at college with a keen interest in linguistics and its applications to real-world issues, arrived.
(Subject = *Ashwin*, and everything that modifies the subject; predicate = *arrived*)

Chapter 2

Identify the helping verbs and main verbs in the following sentences. For main verbs, also decide if they are action or linking verbs.

Where has Elana been all day?
(*has* = helping verb; *been* = main verb/linking)

Tie your shoes, Morgan!
(*tie* = main verb/action)

Maria was absent on Thursday.
(*was* = main verb/linking; *absent* = adjective)

Weon Woo is conducting research.
(*is* = helping; *conducting* = main/action)

Amanda's been studying Theatre Arts in college.
(*has been* = helping verbs; *studying* = main/action)

Note that even though *been* is a form of *to be*, it's not acting as a linking verb here.

Chapter 3

Identify the verb forms in the following sentences and explain why those forms are being used.

Felix has earned several promotions over the years.
(Present perfect = happened several unspecified times in the past. Compare to *Felix earned his promotions in 2005 and 2008*, where the simple past is used for specified times in the past.)

The forensic linguists are working on the case.
(Present progressive = happening now and on-going)

Taran was laughing loudly when the children entered the room.
(*was laughing* is in the past progressive = on-going in the past when another activity interrupted; *entered*, in the simple past)

Lin has lived in New York for 10 years.
(Present perfect = occurred in the past and still true. Compare to *Lin lived in New York for 10 years* = Lin lives elsewhere now.)

It will have stopped raining by the time we arrive at the stadium.
(Future perfect is used to order two events in the future. The stopping of
the rain will happen before we arrive, which is in the simple present.)

Keisha had purchased the computer two days before the prices soared.
(Past perfect, to order two events in the past. Because of the word *before*,
we could make do with two simple past verbs as well.)

Chapter 4

The following sentences have non-standard subject–verb pairings.
Change to the standard forms.

*This set of self-reported reactions to potentially dangerous situations have
generally been found to be quite accurate.*
(Grammatical subject = *set*, singular; takes verb *has*)

There's five letters I have to send before noon.
(The word that agrees with the verb = *letters*, plural; takes verb *are*)

Jamal or I are going to be called to the board next.
(*or* is the conjunction in the subject, so the closest word, *I*, agrees with
the verb; takes verb *am*. If the construction *Jamal or I am going . . .*
sounds odd to you, reword the sentence.)

Everyone living with a lot of cats need to stock up on lint rollers.
(Subject = *everyone*, singular; takes verb *needs*)

Neither of the shops hire after the holiday rush.
(Subject = *neither*, singular; takes verb *hires*)

Chapter 5

What about the following sentence is not standard grammar?

Ryan drinks five sodas a day.
(*Soda* is officially a mass noun. The standard wording would be *cans* (or *bottles*) *of soda*. In this example, however, the wording could imply that Ryan makes a point of drinking different brands (or flavors) of sodas daily. Being explicit about the unit of measurement would make the meaning clearer.)

Identify any gerunds and infinitives in the following sentences. Not all sentences have gerunds and/or infinitive verbs.

Learning to swim is a basic requirement of summer camp.
(*learning* = gerund; *to swim* = infinitive)

To find happiness is your main task.
(*To find* = infinitive)

Struggling with a lot of debt, the business finally closed.
(none; *struggling* is a present participle but not being used as a noun)

The children like to watch TV in the morning.
(*to watch* = infinitive)

Chapter 6

Identify any direct and indirect objects in the following sentences.

Felicia sent a letter to Janna.
(*a letter* = direct object; *Janna* = indirect object)

Janna gave Taylor the letter next.
(*Taylor* = indirect object; *the letter* = direct object)

Taylor read the letter on the bus.
(*letter* = direct object; *bus* is not indirect object in that it doesn't indirectly benefit from the action. It is the object of the preposition.)

Can dative movement happen in the sentences above? In other words, can you have the double object construction, with the indirect object before the direct object?

Felicia sent Janna a letter = yes, dative movement can happen.
Janna gave Taylor the letter next = dative movement has already happened.

Taylor read the letter on the bus = no, dative movement can't happen when there is no indirect object.

Do the following sentences contain complements? If so, what types?

Chris thought the children bright.
(Yes, direct object complement of the adjectival type. Note that you can say *Chris thought the children <u>to be</u> bright.*)

Chris taught the children music.
(No. Can't say *Chris taught the children <u>to be</u> music.* Music = direct object; children = indirect object)

Chris seems to be a patient teacher.
(Yes, subject complement of the noun phrase type: *a patient teacher* is a noun phrase)

Chapter 7

The following sentences include non-standard uses of verbs. Discuss what is non-standard about their use.

The plan impacts our economy.

(The word *impact* used to be only a noun. Lately, it has taken on the role of a transitive verb: *to impact something.* In fact, such usage might now qualify as standard, just!)

Harriet graduated high school last year.

(The verb *to graduate* is generally an intransitive verb, so you would say *someone graduated from* a school. As with *impact*, the transitivity of *to graduate* is in flux.)

Marsha laid on the couch yesterday, doing nothing.

(Past tense of *to lie*, intransitive, is *lay*, so *Marsha lay on the couch yesterday.*)

Chapter 8

Check to see if the verb forms in the following sentences are using the subjunctive in a standard way.

If you won the lottery, you will be rich.

(Verb in past tense in the "if clause," so need not *will* but *would* = hypothetical conditional)

If I was you, I'd start the term paper tonight.

(It's not possible for I to be you, so need subjunctive *were*)

If I was cooking dinner tonight, I'd make pasta.

(It might happen, so don't need subjunctive)

Lee is adamant that her best friend sits next to her.

(The current wording is not in the subjunctive. However, since the message in the sentence is a wish (a strong wish), we want the unconjugated *sit*, and hence need *Lee is adamant that her best friend* _sit_ next to her. My grammar checker is suggesting _sits_, so there's another blot on the subjunctive.)

Chapter 9

Passivize the following sentences and identify the tense of the active versions:

Anin has tutored Mayra once a week all term.
(_Mayra has been tutored by Anin_ = present perfect tense is preserved)

Karina is reading the new best-seller.
(_The new best-seller is being read by Karina_ = –ing ending now on the inserted helping verb; present progressive)

Put the following sentences back into their active forms:
Adam was spotted by his fans.
(_His fans spotted Adam_ = the active sentence has no helping verb; simple past)

Zena has been being observed by her boss.
(_Her boss has been observing Zena_ = this passive sentence might seem odd to you, too many _be_'s perhaps. While it is the passivized form of the active sentence counterpart in the present perfect progressive, most people would instead probably prefer _Zena has been observed by her boss_ or _Zena is being observed by her boss_.)

Chapter 10

Evaluate the use of pronouns in these sentences:

The results were positive for Barbara and I.
(*for Barbara and me* = *me* is one of the objects of the preposition *for*)

If it's me they want, that's who they'll get.
(*If it's me they want, that's whom they'll get* = even though both pronouns are after the verb *to be*, they should be in the objective case since they are direct objects. *They want [me]* and *they'll get [me]*; *me* is fine; *who* should be *whom*.)

Did you hear who Andrea bought tickets from? She's an old elementary school pal of mine who I haven't seen in years.
(*Who* or *whom*? *Andrea bought tickets from [whom]*; *I haven't seen [whom] in years.* Both instances call for the objective case *whom*.)

Chapter 11

Identify the adjectives and adverbs in the following sentences and explain what they modify. Convert any non-standard forms to the standard.

Don't speak too loud in the office.
(*loudly* = adverb modifying *speak*)

Rosemary is a very speedy typist.
(*very* = adverb modifying adjective *speedy*; *speedy* = adjective modifying noun *typist*)

She writes worse than a pre-schooler.
(*worse* = adverb modifying verb *writes*)

Her penmanship is worse than a doctor's.
(*worse* = adjective modifying noun *penmanship*)

She types well, however.
(*well* = adverb modifying the verb *types*)

I am well.
(*well* = here it's an adjective used to describe the subject pronoun *I*, in the sense of well-being)

I'm good.
(*good* is being used in an informal way; *well* would be the standard adjective if being asked about one's well-being. *I'm good* is also used (in the US) to mean *No thank you* if asked by a host if we want anything or if everything is okay; and can be heard in self-congratulatory exclamations after accomplishments in such utterances as, *Damn, I'm good!*)

Apple has the slogan "Think Different." Is this grammatical?
(Technically, no. Adverb *differently* should modify verb *think*. Apple has said, though, that *different* is being used as a direct object, as in "Think Computers." There is also an analogy to "Be Different," where an adjective works.)

Chapter 12

Is the underlined word a preposition or a verb particle? (Hint, if it's a particle, you'll be able to move it and the sentence will remain well formed.)

We have sent <u>out</u> all the letters.
(Particle; can move; phrasal verb = *to send out*)

Several people brought <u>up</u> that topic.
(Particle; can move; phrasal verb = *to bring up*)

Shauna slid <u>off</u> her chair.
(Preposition; cannot move; prepositional phrase = *off her chair*)

The plane flew <u>over</u> the North Pole.
(Preposition; cannot move; prepositional phrase = *over the North Pole*)

Keith will leave <u>on</u> the 12th.
(Preposition; cannot move; prepositional phrase = *on the 12th*)

Chapter 13

Identify the conjunction type and the sentence type in the following sentences:

Monica plays the banjo but never in front of an audience.
(Coordinating conjunction, *but* used in phrasal way; simple sentence)

Suzy plays the drums, and her kit is in the basement.
(Coordinating conjunction, *and* used in the sentential way; compound sentence)

Katie plays the piano since her parents are very musical, and she is grateful for their support.
(We have a compound-complex sentence here: subordinating conjunction *since* and coordinating conjunction *and* used in a sentential way)

Chapter 14

Evaluate the use of relative pronouns in the following sentences. Convert any non-standard to standard forms.

Carissa decided to take the class which meets on Mondays.
(If the specific class is not in doubt, we could use non-restrictive *which*, but we'll need a comma before it. More likely, this sentence is giving us information about one class out of several possibilities, and we would want restrictive *that* = *Carissa decided to take the class that meets on Mondays*; no comma.)

Brian chats with friends that have Facebook accounts.
(The antecedent of the relative pronoun is *friends* – animate; *that* sounds odd to me – I prefer *who* and *whom* for people.)

Loren knows that the secret is in the box.
(The sentence is fine, but note that the word *that* functions as a complementizer, not a relative pronoun; *that the secret is in the box* is a complement clause.)

Brooklyn, that is the most crowded borough, is home to Prospect Park.
(*that* should be *which*; keep commas. There is no confusion about which Brooklyn we are talking about, so we don't need to restrict the pool. We want a non-restrictive relative clause starting with *which*.)

The recording sounded best was a vinyl album.
(This sentence has a reduced relative clause, but some relative clauses can't reduce. In the full relative clause *that sounded best*, the relative pronoun is the subject of the relative clause and it's not followed by *to be*. Remember you can delete a relative pronoun when it is followed by the subject of the relative clause. When it <u>is</u> the subject of the relative clause, and not followed by *to be*, it must be present; we need to put the relative pronoun *that* back in.)

Chapter 15

Identify what type of phrase might be misplaced in the following sentences, and correct the wording of the sentence.

Floating in the soup, Treb found a bug.
(Present participle phrase; *Treb found a bug floating in the soup.*)

Floating in the pool, Treb felt relaxed.
(Nothing is misaligned here.)

Written ages ago, the author dusted off the manuscript.
(Past participle phrase; *The author dusted off the manuscript that was written ages ago.*)

Chapter 16

The following sentences have incorrect punctuation. Correct any errors and explain what was wrong.

Charlie plays pool every Thursday. Something he enjoys.
(The second half is a sentence fragment. Need a comma after *Thursday*.)

Sharon also likes to play pool, however, she never has the free time to get to the pool hall.
(Comma splice/run-on. *However* is a conjunctive adverb. Need period or semi-colon after *pool*.)

They should form a team. The reason being that they are so talented.
(This is a common sentence fragment error. The second part doesn't have a finite verb supplying information about time, person, and number. Need comma after *team*.)

Chapter 17

Fix the incorrect use of apostrophes in the sentences below.

The name of a Lucille Ball movie from the 1960's is "You'rs, Mine and Our's."
(*1960s* = you don't need an apostrophe for plural. *Yours, Mine and Ours* = no apostrophes needed for possessive pronouns; note also that the serial comma isn't used in the title, or in the remake from 2005.)

Womens' shoes are on the fourth floor.
(Look to the left of the apostrophe; *womens* is not a word. We want *women's*.)

The Number 6 Bus' wheels have fallen off.
(*Bus's* if you go with the rule that a possessive that adds a syllable to the base form needs that extra *s*)

Who's vs. *Whose?* Fill in the blanks.

___ *book is this?*
(*Whose* = possessive)

___ *at the door?*
(*Who's* = contraction)

Cheat Sheet tables

Table A: Verb form matrix (2)[1]

Verb	Simple present	Simple past	Present participle	Past participle
To eat	eat/eats	ate	eating	eaten
To walk	walk/walks	walked	walking	walked
To be	am/is/are	was/were	being	been

Table B: Person–number matrix (2)

	Singular	Plural
First person	I	we
Second person	you	you
Third person	he/she/it	they

Table C: Verb forms of "to go" (3)

	Simple	Progressive	Perfect
Present	go/goes	am/is/are going	has/have gone
Past	went	was/were going	had gone
Future	will go	will be going	will have gone

Table D: Verb forms in progressive, present/past/future (3)

I am walking. I was walking. I will be walking.

You are walking. You were walking. You will be walking.

He/She/It is walking. He/She/It was walking. He/She/It will be walking.

We are walking. We were walking. We will be walking.

You (plural) are walking. You were walking. You will be walking.

They are walking. They were walking. They will be walking.

[1] Chapter number in which material is discussed.

Cheat Sheet tables

Table E: Verb forms in perfect, present/past/future (3)

I have walked. I had walked. I will have walked.

You have walked. You had walked. You will have walked.

He/She/It has walked. He/She/It had walked. He/She/It will have walked.

We have walked. We had walked. We will have walked.

You (plural) have walked. You had walked. You will have walked.

They have walked. They had walked. They will have walked.

Table F: Common situations that result in non-standard subject–verb agreement (4)

When the subject and the verb are separated

When the subject contains a conjunction (*and*, *or*)

When the subject's number is ambiguous

When the subject doesn't really agree with the verb

When the verb of agreement is a modal verb

When the sentence mood is subjunctive or imperative

Table G: Quantifiers with count and mass nouns (5)

Quantifier	Count noun	Quantifier	Mass noun
many	*many dollar bills*	much	*much money*
fewer	*fewer dimes*	less	*less change*
number	*number of loans*	amount	*amount of debt*

Table H: Determiner categories and examples (5)

Pre-determiner alone: *all cats, both cats, most cats*

Pre-determiner and regular determiner: *all of the cats, both of the cats, most of the cats*

Regular determiner alone: *those cats, my cats*

Regular and post-determiner: *the five cats, the fifth cat*

Q: Comparative and superlative adjectives and adverbs (11)

...ives modify nouns and pronouns.

...bs modify verbs, adjectives, and other adverbs.

...ck is *slow*. He is *slower* than Denise. He is *the slowest* person I know.

... = adjective modifying noun *Derrick* and pronoun *he*.

...ise walks *quickly*. She walks *more quickly* than Derrick. She walks *the most quickly* of ...one I know.

...ickly = adverb modifying verb *walks*.

...e is *very fast*.

...ery = adverb modifying adjective *fast*.

...he jogs *very quickly*.

...ery = adverb modifying adverb *quickly*.

Table R: Coordinating conjunctions and meanings (13)

Here are the seven coordinating conjunctions (BOYSFAN words) and their meanings.

But = opposite
Or = alternative
Yet = opposite
So = cause/effect
For = because
And = addition, progression
Nor = negative of *or*

Table S: Subordinating conjunctions (13)

Here are many of the commonly used subordinating conjunctions, categorized by type of information being conveyed.

Causality (*because, so that, since*)
Possibility (*if, unless, whether*)
Time (*before, after, when, while*)
Contrast (*although, even though*)

Post-determiners alone: *10 hilarious cats*

Pre- and post-determiner: *all 10 cats*

Using all determiner types: *all of the 10 hilarious cats*

Table I: Summary of the various behaviors of direct object (DO) and indirect object (IO) (6)

Base form:
Tony baked a cake for Sam: DO, then IO in the prepositional phrase

Dative movement allowed (double object construction):
Tony baked Sam a cake: IO before DO

Dative movement not allowed:
Tony washed the car for Sam: DO before IO
*Tony washed Sam the car: can't have IO before DO
*Tony baked Sam it: DO is a pronoun

IO is also object of preposition:
Tony washed the car for Sam.
Harry cooked dinner for Fred.
Mathilda danced for the audience.

No IO; only object of preposition:
Harry cooked dinner for the weekend.
Beth read the book on the subway.

No DO; only IO (with preposition)
Harry cooked for Fred.

No DO; only IO (without preposition)
Harry texted Fred.

Table J: Complement types identified by part of sentence being described (6)

Subject complements

Predicate noun: *Allen is a mathematician*.

Predicate adjective: *Ali is fabulous*.

Direct object complements

Predicate noun: *Jerry appoints the shy student <u>attendance monitor</u>.*

Predicate adjective: *Shelby considers her friends <u>loyal</u>.*

Table K: Complement types identified by part of speech in complement position: (6)

Predicate nouns

Subject complement: *Allen is <u>a mathematician</u>.*

Direct object complement: *Jerry appoints the shy student <u>attendance monitor</u>.*

Predicate adjectives

Subject complement: *Ali is <u>fabulous</u>.*

Direct object complement: *Shelby considers her friends <u>loyal</u>.*

Table L: Verb forms of verbs *to lie* and *to lay* (7)

Triplets of confusable lie/lay in infinitive/simple present/simple past/past participle

To lie	lie(s)/lay/lain = intransitive (place oneself parallel to a surface)
To lay	lay(s)/laid/laid = transitive (place something down)
To lie	lie(s)/lied/lied = intransitive (not tell the truth)

Table M: Uses of the subjunctive mood (8)

The subjunctive mood is used to convey the following meanings:

- Contrary to fact or hypothetical: *If I <u>were</u> you, I would go home. <u>Were</u> it not for his dog, David would never take walks.*
- Something in doubt: *If this treaty <u>were</u> signed, there would be peace.*
- Something for which you are (or were, or will be) wishing: *I asked that Corinne <u>be</u> here by 9 am.*
- In idioms: *If need <u>be</u>; far <u>be</u> it from me [to do something].*

Table N: Personal pronouns by case (10)

Nominative case	Objective case	Possessive case
I	me	my/mine
you	you	your/yours
he	him	his/his
she	her	her/hers
it	it	its/its
we	us	our/ours
you (pl.)	you (pl.)	your/yours (pl.)
they	them	their/theirs

Table O: Reflexive pronouns (10)

	Singular	Plural
First person	myself	ourselves
Second person	yourself	yourselves
Third person	himself/herself/itself	themselves

Table P: *Who/whom* tips (10)

Use *who*
- when the word is the subject of a sentence or clause.
- if the next word in the sentence is a verb.

Use *whom*
- when the word is the direct object of the sentence or clause.
- when the word is the indirect object of the sentence or clause.
- when the word is the object in a prepositional phrase.
- if the next word in the sentence is a noun.
- if the next word in an interrogative is a helping verb.

Cheat Sheet tables

Table T: Conjunction usage and sentence types (13)

Coordinating conjunctions being used in a phrasal way = simple sentence
(example = *Roger played tennis and golf on the same day.*)

Coordinating conjunctions being used in a sentential way = compound sentence
(example = *Shane played dominos, and Shauna kept score.*)

Subordinating conjunctions where dependent clause is first = complex sentence
(example = *Whenever Maureen practices the trombone, her dog hides.*)

Subordinating conjunctions where independent clause is first = also complex sentence
(example = *The dog knows to hide whenever Maureen takes out her trombone.*)

Table U: Subject relative clauses (14)

Restrictive: *The prize that is worth $2000 is a trip to Hawaii.* (There are several prizes, and we limit which one we are talking about)

Non-restrictive: *The prize, which is worth $2000, is a trip to Hawaii.* (There is only one possible prize being discussed)

Table V: Object relative clauses (14)

Restrictive: *Jake won the prize that was donated by Mr. Howell.*

Non-restrictive: *Jake won the prize, which was donated by Mr. Howell.*

Table W: Uses of the comma (16)

Rule 1: Use a comma right before a coordinating conjunction (BOYSFAN word) when the conjunction is linking two independent clauses in a compound sentence; in other words, when it is being used sententially. If it's being used phrasally, don't use a comma.

Rule 2: Use a comma after a dependent clause when an independent clause follows in a complex sentence. If the independent clause comes first, don't use a comma.

Rule 3: Use commas to set apart a non-restrictive relative clause from the main sentence. Do not use commas to separate a restrictive relative clause from the main sentence.

Rule 4: Use commas when listing.

Rule 5: Use a comma after introductory material in a sentence that delays the subject.

Cheat Sheet tables

Rule 6: Use commas to set off parenthetical information (unless you are using parentheses).

Rule 7: Use commas to set off an appositive, i.e. extra identifying information about an entity already mentioned in the sentence.

Rule 8: Use commas to set off direct address material.

Rule 9: Use commas in dates.

Rule 10: Use commas in addresses.

Rule 11: Use commas with a series of adjectives, but not after the last adjective in the list.

Rule 12: Use a comma before quoted material.

Table X: Apostrophe use (17)

Signal possession
Possessive on singular noun
The girl's coat

Possessive on plural noun
The girls' basketball team

Possessive on noun with added syllable
The boss's orders

Possessive pronouns (no apostrophe)
The book is hers; the photo is theirs

Signal contraction
It's = it is, it has
Won't = will not

Signal some plural forms
Oona is spelled with two o's.
Don't forget to count all the um's in his speech.

Glossary

Action verb Verb conveying an action, as opposed to a state of being.

Active voice Sentence construction in which the agent is in the subject slot, usually at the start of the sentence.

Adjectival clause Part of a sentence with a subject–verb pair, acting as an adjective.

Adjectival phrase Part of a sentence without a subject–verb pair, acting as an adjective.

Adjectival possessive pronoun Pronoun in the possessive case, acting as a determiner to the following noun.

Adjective Part of speech modifying a noun or pronoun.

Adverb Word modifying a verb, adjective, or other adverb.

Adverbial clause Part of a sentence with a subject–verb pair, acting as an adverb.

Adverbial phrase Part of a sentence without a subject–verb pair, acting as an adverb.

Agent Entity in a sentence carrying out some action.

Agentless passive Sentence in the passive voice lacking the prepositional phrase that would have conveyed the entity carrying out the action (the agent).

Antecedent Word or phrase that conveys the referent of a pronoun.

Appositive Phrase that conveys additional identifying information about an entity in the sentence.

Aspect Information about the duration of an event, conveyed in verb forms.

Bare infinitive The second half of the infinitive verb, not including the *to*.

Case Information about the role any entity plays in a sentence; conveyed by pronoun forms and possessive marker on nouns.

Clause Group of words containing a subject–verb pair; might or might not be able to stand alone as its own sentence.

Collective noun Noun representing a group; treated grammatically as singular.

Comma splice Punctuation error whereby a comma is used to separate two independent clauses; a type of run-on sentence.

Comparative Form of an adjective or adverb used when evaluating two entities or actions.

Complement Part of the predicate; gives more information about the subject or the direct object; sometimes called a predicate complement.

Complement clause Type of dependent clause made up of a complementizer and following clause; functions as a noun clause.

Complementizer Word that begins a complement clause; usually *that*; can be deleted when reducing a complement clause.

Complex sentence Sentence consisting of an independent clause and a dependent clause.

Compound sentence Sentence consisting of at least two independent clauses joined by a coordinating conjunction.

Compound-complex sentence Sentence consisting of at least two independent clauses and a dependent clause.

Conditional Sentential form that conveys possibility of an action or event, contingent upon the certainty of another action or event; usually an *if/then* meaning conveyed by a sentence containing a present tense verb and the modal *will*; e.g. *If I go, I will enjoy myself.*

Conjugation Change in the form of a verb so that it conveys information about time, as well as information about the subject's number and person.

Conjunction Part of speech that joins clauses and phrases.

Conjunctive adverb Part of speech that conveys the relationship between the independent clauses it joins; punctuation requires a semi-colon or period.

Contraction Word constructed from two words being merged; often with spelling and pronunciation modification.

Coordinating conjunction Part of speech that joins two independent clauses in its sentential function; joins smaller parts of a sentence in its phrasal function.

Copula verb The verb *to be*.

Count noun Noun that can take a plural marker.

Dative movement Sentence transformation whereby the indirect object moves up in the sentence to precede the direct object, creating a double object construction; only occurs with certain verbs; doesn't occur when the direct object is a pronoun.

Declarative sentence Sentence conveying a statement.

Demonstrative pronoun Pronoun pointing to an entity: *this*, *that*, *these*, *those*.

Dependent clause Part of a sentence that contains a subject–verb pair but cannot stand alone as its own sentence, e.g. a relative clause, a complement clause, or a clause starting with a subordinating conjunction

Determiner Part of speech that precedes a noun; there are pre-, regular, and post-determiners.

Direct object Entity directly benefiting from the verb in a sentence.

Direct object complement of the adjectival type Information in the complement of a sentence's predicate that modifies the direct object of the sentence with an adjective.

Direct object complement of the noun phrase type Information in the complement of a sentence's predicate that restates or modifies the direct object of the sentence with a noun phrase.

Ditransitive verb Verb that requires both a direct and an indirect object.

Dummy subject Word that fills in the subject slot in a sentence but has no semantic value, e.g. *there*, *it*; sometimes called expletive.

Exclamatory mood Sentence form that conveys a statement exclaiming/proclaiming something.

Glossary

Finite verb Verb form conjugated for information about time, number, and person.

Full verb Part of a sentence consisting of any helping verb(s) and the main verb.

Fused sentence Punctuation error created by two independent clauses without any punctuation mark at the junction; a type of run-on sentence.

Future tense Verb form conveying time information about an action still to come.

Gerund Noun that has been formed from the bare infinitive of a verb with an *–ing* suffix.

Helping verb Verb that precedes the main verb in a full verb and conveys information about time, number, and person; also called an auxiliary verb.

Hypothetical conditional Sentence form conveying an *if/then* meaning, containing a past tense verb and the modal *would, could,* or *might*; e.g. *If I went to the party, then I would bring some cake.*

Hypothetical future Sentence form conveying possibility, using the modal verbs *would* or *could* but no *if*-clause; e.g. *What would you buy with a million dollars?*

Imperative mood Sentence form with implied subject *you* and bare infinitive, conveying a command.

Indefinite pronoun Pronoun whose antecedent is not explicit; e.g. *someone, something.*

Independent clause Group of words containing a subject–verb pair that can stand alone as its own sentence.

Indicative mood Sentence form conveying a statement.

Indirect object Entity indirectly benefiting from the verb in a sentence; direct recipient of the direct object.

Infinitive verb Nonfinite verb form not conjugated for information about time, number, or person; consists of the word *to* and the bare infinitive.

Infinitive verb phrase Infinitive verb and modifying words; can act as a noun.

Informal passive Sentence construction whereby the passive verb form uses the verb *to get* instead of the copula *to be* as the helping verb; main verb still in the past participle.

Interrogative mood Sentence form asking a question.

Interrogative pronoun Pronoun used in the interrogative mood, specifically with wh-interrogatives: *who, whom, whose,* and *what.*

Intransitive verb Verb that does not allow a direct object to follow.

Irregular verb Verb whose conjugation does not follow the regular formula, e.g. does not take the *–ed* suffix for the past tense.

Linking verb Verb that links the subject to information about the subject; usually the copula verb *to be.*

Main verb Primary verb in a sentence; in a full verb, comes after a helping verb.

Mass noun Noun that does not take a plural marker.

Misaligned modifier Modifying phrase or clause that is either not accurately aligned with the entity it is modifying in a sentence (misplaced modifier) or has no such entity in the sentence (dangling modifier).

Modal verb Helping verb that conveys the mood (intent) of the speaker; is not conjugated for number and person.

Mood Sentence meaning conveying the intent of the speaker; exclamatory, imperative, indicative, interrogative, and subjunctive; can be signaled by verb forms, implied subject *you,* etc.

Negation Sentence structure that conveys a negative or opposite meaning.

Nominal possessive pronoun Possessive pronoun that takes the place of both the possessor and the possessed, e.g. in *That new car is hers, hers = her + car.*

Nominative case Form of a pronoun conveying the word's status as subject of a clause.

Nonfinite verb Verb form not conjugated for information about time, number, and person: present participle, past participle, and infinitive verb.

Non-restrictive relative clause Type of dependent clause; starts with a relative pronoun and does not restrict the pool of possible entities being discussed; when choosing between relative pronouns *which* and *that*, the non-restrictive clause takes *which*; commas separate the clause from the rest of the sentence.

Noun Word that represents an entity; may be subject, direct object, indirect object, object of a preposition, or complement.

Noun clause Part of a sentence with a subject–verb pair that functions as a noun.

Noun phrase Noun (or its associated pronoun) and any modifying words; does not include a subject–verb pair; functions as would a noun.

Number Information signaling *singular* or *plural*, conveyed on nouns, pronouns, and some verbs.

Object Word that represents an entity that is receiving the action of the sentence, either directly or indirectly, or as the second part of a prepositional phrase.

Object relative clause Type of dependent clause that gives extra information about an object in the main sentence.

Objective case Form of a pronoun conveying the word's status as an object, either direct object, indirect object, or object of a prepositional phrase.

Particle movement Sentence transformation that moves the particle of a phrasal verb to the end of the sentence, e.g. *Please turn the heat up.*

Passive voice Sentence construction in which the entity directly benefiting from the verb (direct object) is in the subject slot, usually at the start of the sentence.

Past participle Nonfinite verb form that is the third of a verb's triplets (*eat/ate/eaten*); functions as an adjective, main verb in the perfect verb form with helping verb *to have*, and main verb in the passive voice construction with helping verb *to be*.

Past participle phrase Part of a sentence without a subject–verb pair that includes the past participle form of a verb and any related material.

Perfect progressive verb form Verb form that includes both present participle and past participle to emphasize duration of an action.

Perfect verb form Verb form comprising the helping verb *to have* and a main verb in the past participle; conveys time information about actions that have been completed in relation to other actions or at unspecified times.

Person Information on nouns, pronouns, and some verbs; *first person* signals the speaker; *second person* signals the listener; *third person* signals a third party not directly involved in the communicative exchange.

Personal pronoun Pronoun whose antecedent is a known entity.

Phrasal verb A two-part verb consisting of a main verb and a particle; the particle itself consists of one (sometimes two) prepositions, e.g. *to turn up*.

Phrase Group of words without a subject–verb pair; cannot stand alone as a sentence.

Possessive case Form of a noun or pronoun conveying the fact that the entity owns/possesses something; with nouns, usually signaled with "apostrophe *s*."

Predicate Part of the sentence that contains the helping and/or main verb, as well as all information that modifies the verb.

Preposition Word conveying information about time, location, or some metaphorical relationship.

Prepositional phrase Part of a sentence consisting of (minimally) a preposition and its object: either a noun, noun phrase, or pronoun; including any words that modify the object.

Present participle Nonfinite verb form consisting of a bare infinitive verb and an *-ing* suffix; functions as a gerund, adjective, and main verb in the progressive verb form with helping verb *to be*.

Present participle phrase Part of a sentence without a subject–verb pair that includes a verb in the present participle form (with *–ing* suffix) and any related material.

Progressive verb form Verb form comprising the helping verb *to be* and a main verb with *–ing* suffix (the present participle); used to emphasize an on-going activity in the past, present, or future.

Pronoun Word that functions as a substitute for an antecedent: the antecedent conveys more exact information about the pronoun.

Pseudo question Clause with declarative subject–verb word order but interrogative meaning.

Quantifier A modifying word conveying information about the quantity of an entity.

Reciprocal pronoun Pronoun conveying an exchange: *each other* for exchange between two parties; *one another* for exchange among three or more.

Reduced relative clause Type of dependent clause giving extra information about an entity in the main sentence; such clauses are reduced when the relative pronoun (and sometimes the following copula verb) is deleted.

Reflexive pronoun Pronoun with the suffix *–self* or *–selves*; reflecting back on an antecedent in the same clause; sometimes used for emphasis.

Regular verb Verb whose conjugation follows the usual formula, e.g. for past tense, add *–ed* suffix.

Relative clause Type of dependent clause beginning with a relative pronoun and giving extra information about an entity in the main clause. Relative clauses can modify the subject or direct object of the main clause; they can be restrictive and non-restrictive; and they can be full or reduced.

Relative pronoun Pronoun beginning a relative clause: *who, whom, whose, which,* and *that*.

Restrictive relative clause Type of dependent clause; starts with a relative pronoun and narrows the pool of possible entities being discussed; when the choice of relative pronoun is *which* or *that*, the restrictive relative clause takes *that*; no commas are needed to separate the clause from the rest of the sentence.

Run-on sentence Punctuation error whereby two independent clauses are not separated by the correct punctuation mark. A fused sentence is formed from the absence of any punctuation at the junction; a comma splice is formed from the use of a comma at the junction.

Semi-colon Punctuation mark that separates two independent clauses, signaling a closer relationship between the clauses than would a period; also used instead of commas to separate entries in lists when entries in the list have their own internal comma.

Sentence fragment Group of words that does not contain enough information to stand alone as a sentence.

Sentential adverb Adverb at the beginning of a sentence that modifies the whole sentence rather than a particular verb, adjective, or other adverb.

Serial comma Comma used in between the next-to-last and last entry in a list.

Simple past tense Verb form with no helping verb, conveying the fact that the action happened in the past.

Simple present tense Verb form with no helping verb, conveying the fact that the action happens in the present or is habitual.

Simple sentence Sentence consisting of a single independent clause.

Simple subject Noun or pronoun in the subject position of the sentence without any modifying or related words.

Simple verb The main verb in a sentence without a helping verb or any modifying or related words.

Split infinitive Structure in which a modifying word, usually an adverb, is placed between the two parts of the infinitive verb: *to* and the bare infinitive.

Glossary

Stative verb Verb expressing state of being, either emotional, mental, or involving the senses.

Subject Noun or pronoun, usually in the first slot in the sentence; in active voice sentences, also the agent of the action.

Subject complement of the adjectival type Information in the complement of a sentence's predicate that modifies the subject of the sentence with an adjective.

Subject complement of the noun phrase type Information in the complement of a sentence's predicate that restates or modifies the subject of the sentence with a noun phrase.

Subject relative clause Type of dependent clause that gives extra information about the subject of the main clause.

Subject–verb agreement Requirement that the number and person of the subject be matched by the appropriate verb form.

Subjunctive mood Verb form that conveys information about some situation that is contrary to fact or hypothetical, something in doubt, something wished for; also occurs in certain idioms.

Subordinating conjunction Word that conveys information about causality, possibility, time, or contrast, e.g. *because*, *since*, *if*, *while*, *although*. When placed at the beginning of an independent clause, it makes that clause dependent. A complex sentence is formed when such a dependent clause (starting with a subordinating conjunction) joins with an independent clause.

Superlative Form of an adjective or adverb used when evaluating three or more entities or actions.

Tense Time information conveyed by the form of a verb.

Tense jumping Transformation undergone by certain sentence structures (e.g. passive voice, negation) whereby the tense marking on the main verb moves onto an adjacent helping verb.

Transitive verb Verb that requires a direct object.

Vague pronoun Pronoun whose antecedent is ambiguous or unknown.

Verb Part of speech that conveys action or state of being, and may be conjugated for information about time, number, and person.

Verb particle The second half of a phrasal verb, consisting of one (or more) prepositions.

Wh-interrogative Sentence in the interrogative mood that asks a question with a sentence-initial *wh*-word, the answer to which requires information; sometimes called an *information question*.

Yes–no interrogative Sentence in the interrogative mood that asks a question, the answer to which is *yes* or *no*.

Index

Page numbers in **bold** refer to figures, page numbers in *italic* refer to tables.

Index

Index

Index